TILDA

A REASON TO BE

LIVING OUT YOUR LIFE PURPOSE

VOLUME 3

A REASON TO BE

A REASON TO BE

Printed in the United States of America

Copyright @ 2019 Tilda Whitaker

ISBN-13: 978-0-9998789-3-4
Library of Congress Cataloging-in-Publication Data

The copyright laws of the United States of America protect this book. No part of this publication may be reproduced or stored in a retrieval system for commercial gain or profit.

No part of this publication may be stored electronically or otherwise transmitted in any form or by any means- for example, electronic, photocopy, recording- without written permission of the author.

Scripture quotations are taken from the Holy Bible, King James Version, copyright © 1996, 2004, 2007, 2013, 2015 by Tyndale House Foundation. All rights reserved.

Book Coaching & Editing by:
SynergyEd Consulting/ www.synergyedconsulting.com

Cover Design: Erica Green
Graphics & Marketing: Greenlight Creations- glightcreations.com
Photography: Jerrell Jordan

SHERO PUBLISHING
Impressing the World, One Book At A Time

Published by: SHERO PUBLISHING
SHEROPublishing.com
For copies and publishing information, email: ericaperrygreen@gmail.com

---

Be it advised that all information within this literary work, *A Reason To Be*, has been acknowledged to be the truthful account of each author. The authors are responsible for the content in their individual chapter and hold Shero Publishing harmless for any legal action arising as a result of their participation in this publication.

A REASON TO BE

LIVING OUT YOUR LIFE PURPOSE

15 AUTHORS SHARING THEIR
PURPOSE JOURNEY

VOLUME 3

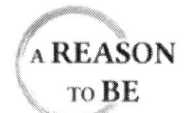

Table of Contents

DEDICATION	6
ACKNOWLEDGMENT	7
Nora Weeto Adamu *Letting Go*	8
Tracey Aiken *Love Beyond Your Perspective*	18
Regal Cameron *Journey to Purpose*	30
Marlene Fuller *Your Setbacks Are Just Setups*	42
Erica Perry Green *Not My Plan, But HIS!*	54
Sandra Hardy *From Molestation to Purpose*	64
Tammie Harris *Rags to True Riches*	76
Teresa Howard *My Pain Became My Purpose*	86
Dr. Peggy Jones *What's Going on In This House?*	92
Richard Joyner *The Land of Reason*	104
Rhonda P Kaalund *Happiness is a Choice*	114
Jo Ellen Reams *Rise Above It, No Matter What*	124
Dr Marvin Smith *A Reason To Be: Creativity & Innovation*	134
Sheila Spencer *Take The Leap and Let Go*	144
Jacqueline Thompson *My Reason To Be*	152

Dedication

This book continues in the series of *A REASON TO BE* as VOL 3 and is dedicated to the millions of people in the universe who find themselves struggling to find their life purpose.

Acknowledgments

I am grateful to those who supported and encouraged me as I worked on this God given assignment.

Thank you to all the phenomenal authors who participated in this book compilation by sharing your testimonies and expertise to empower and inspire readers globally, to tap into their God-given purpose and their *reason to be*!

Author Nora Weeto Adamu

Nora Weeto Adamu

Born in Yekepa, Liberia, Nora Weeto Adamu is the founder of WOMEN OF VALUE. She has an Associate degree in French Language and Translation from the University of Cocody. She also has an Associate degree in Theology from the Burning Bush Bible Institute in Abidjan, and a Certified Family Life Coach from the P4 Coaching Institute. She is a preacher, speaker and author. She served as one of the Associate Pastors in her local church, The Global Impact Ministries International in Collingdale, Pennsylvania. She is blessed with both biological and spiritual children.

Letting Go

Letting go is one of the hardest things to do especially when you think about how you were treated; the pain, shame, and hurt you experienced. However, it is mandated that we let go so as to be free. Free in our mind, soul, body, and spirit. There is no way you can be free if you keep holding on to things that you experienced in the past. Roy T. Bennett wrote that, "Once you realize you deserve a bright future, letting go of your dark past is the best choice you will ever make." There is no way you can make better decisions about your future if you keep living in the past. My prayer is that this chapter- *LET GO* will open your eyes to see the danger in not letting go and the benefits of letting go that will set you free from every bondage that you find yourself in.

WHAT DOES IT MEANS TO LET GO?

A lot of people are unable to answer this question, not because they do not know what it means; they are afraid that if they answer the question, they will have to make some compromises or changes regarding the things that hurt them; that they are still holding on to. They fear that they will see life in a different way than they now see it.

Letting go means to *release* someone or something. But it is really easier said than done, to release someone or something that you have struggled with for your whole life! Yes, the letting go is difficult, but the pain and hurt it causes us to keep holding on to things and people who don't care about how we feel, is useless. The bible says, in Isaiah: 43:18-19: *Remember not the former things, nor consider the things of old. Behold I am doing a new thing, now it springs forth, do you not perceive it? I will make a way in the wilderness and rivers in the desert.* For you to be able to experience the new things that are in store for you, you have to go beyond the past that is weighing you down and causing you to be bitter about everything and everyone.

Growing up as a child I had lots of difficult moments that I couldn't just let go of. At the age of fourteen, my parents divorced and my mother left me and my siblings with our Dad. My Dad, having all of the responsibility of providing for his children, had to work seven days a week, so he was always gone. We were left to raise ourselves. There was no one home to tell me how to carry myself as a teenager or a young lady and unfortunately, I ended up being molested and abused. The abuse caused me to make other bad decisions; getting into bad relationships and following friends who were not positive role models. All of my teen age and young adult years were a mess, until I had an encounter with the Lord. Even in those dark moments of my life, the Lord was still with me. Even though I was excited that I was now saved and my life was changing, I started to deal with the pain and hurt of my mother leaving us to be raised on our own. The fact that she was not there for me, having to go through life all alone and having the outcome that I had. I started to question God about why did he allowed me to go through all of what I went through, if he knew he had a plan for me? I was hurt and bitter at my Mom and sometimes even at God. As I grew older, I had the opportunity to ask her why did she leave us and she had her own side of the story to tell me. I began to ask the Lord to heal my heart and allow me to love my Mom again and let go of the pain and hurt that I was going through.

Even when I began to become an adult, those difficult moments became a hindrance for me; keeping me from stepping out in boldness to do that which I was supposed to do. The abuses, betrayals, pain and hurt caused me to put myself in a box and prevented me from enjoying the peace and joy that I needed. As a result, I was unable to do what I felt was best for me. So many people find themselves in this same situation, not because they enjoy it, but because it has become a way of life and they are not willing to set themselves free from that bondage.

You will never realize the danger of not releasing people or letting go of them until you go through another hurt or pain. It is like adding more wood to a fire that was dormant and waking it up. Going through pain and hurt all the time, turns you into a different person; someone that you may not even recognize. If you are not strong enough, you lose yourself. That's the reason why most people end up becoming addicted to drugs or alcohol, sink into depression, become affiliated with gangs, or engage in other negative behaviors. Nobody wants to hold on to their past, but situations and circumstances push them into just adapting attitudes and coping mechanisms that are not appropriate. Then there are those who say, "Let go, and let God." Again, this is easier said than done, but because we are children of a God who forgives and forgets, we can do the same because we are made in his image. God can show us how to let go.

As a Certified Family Life Coach, I am walking in my *REASON TO BE*, helping to guide others through the steps of Letting Go and Releasing Their Past. As this is what GOD has ordained for me to do, I want to leave you with the steps to release the shackles off your life and truly Let Go.

HOW DO WE LET GO:

1) **Turn it over to the Lord.**

   Firstly, you must abandon yourself totally into the hands of the Lord. It is sometimes very hard to trust again, when you have been disappointed, looked down upon, disgraced and abused. It takes courage to let go after personal hurts, but know that the Lord is your help. HE is not going to remind you of your past or place guilt on you. The Lord will give you everything that you need. He is going to love you unconditionally and give you a life that you never dreamt of; just trust in him and truly turn it over to GOD.
   Can a mother forget the baby at her breast and have no compassion on the child she has borne? Though she may forget, I will not forget you. Isaiah: 49:15-16

2) **Make the decision to let it go.**
   There is a time to search and a time to give up, and a time to keep and a time to throw away. Ecclesiastes: 3: 6

3) **Surround yourself with positive people.** *Do not be deceived: Bad company ruins good morals.* Corinthians 15:33

4) **Stop blaming others for your failures.**
   Just like in the book of Adam and Eve, Adam wanted to blame Eve for his sins, but had to take accountability. In Genesis 3:12, *Adam said, "The woman you put here with me—she gave me some fruit from the tree, and I ate it."*

5) **Share your story to bless and empower others.**
   How then will they call on him in whom they have not believed? And how are they to believe in him of whom they have never heard? And how are they to hear without someone preaching? Romans: 10:14
   It has seemed good to me to show the signs and wonders that the Most-High God has done for me. Daniel 4:2

A REASON TO BE VOLUME 3

REASONS WHY LETTING GO IS DIFFICULT

1) Hoping that the situation will change.
You cannot start a relationship on a bad foundation and hope that things will get better, because they won't. When your partner has a bad attitude, drinks, cheats, disrespects your family or doesn't consider your thoughts or feelings, see them for who they are the first time. Nothing is going to change, because that is who that person is and you cannot change them, except the Lord choose to.

If the foundation be destroyed, what can the righteous do? (Psalm 11:3) There is nothing you can do when the foundation of what you are doing was not first put in place. Don't get me wrong, the bible says God gives his grace to whom he wants, it could work for X but not for you. Stop having false hope and trust God.

2) The feeling that we were treated wrongly.
One thing we must learn, as Christians, is that as long as we live in the earth we will face lots of challenges. It is the way we handle it that matters. There is nothing new under the heavens. Whatever you find yourself going through today, someone in the bible went through the same thing. Joseph was mistreated by his own brothers and he went through everything that anyone can face on the earth. But at the end of the day, God gave him the victory and he was able to let go of the pain and hurt his brothers costed him. (Genesis: 37-49)

3) Fear that if we walk away it might be the end.
Fear not for I am with you, be not dismayed, for I am your God, I will strengthen you, I will help you, I will uphold you with my righteous right hand. (Isaiah 41:10) With this kind of promise, some people still choose not to trust God, they prefer to listen to people and seek advice everywhere else instead of seeking HIM. At the end of the day, they find themselves alone and still have to make a decision and they are afraid because they did not take the situation to God, who is our present help in time of trouble. Fear will only rape you out of the promises of God for your life and keep you in the same position thinking that you are in the best place. God always has something better in store for us. God promised in Joel: 2:25, that he will restore all of our wasted years and efforts that the enemy did not allow us to enjoy or have.

4) Misinterpreting the real meaning of Love.
There are four different kinds of love, and for you to know what kind you are walking in, you must know them all. If you are not award of the kinds of love you might misunderstand one for another, causing you hurt and pain.

Types of Love:
a) Storge: It is the love that exist between parents and children and between siblings. It is the biblical term in the bible that we are not really familiar with.
b) Philos: It is a love between friends. (Proverbs 17:17)
c) Eros- It is a physical love that exists between two people. Solomon wrote it well. (Song of Solomon 1:2)
d) Agape: This the love that Jesus taught us to walk in; selfless and unconditional, this love allows you to give all of you without wanting anything in return. Often, we mixed all of these four kinds of love together and, at the end of the day, we hurt because we did not choose the right kind of love to walk in.

5) Self Pride
Most of the time, pride prevents us from seeing the truth. We spent more time trying to justify things, than realizing it is time to let go. *For who makes you different from others? What do you have that you did not receive? If then you received it, why do you boast as if you did not receive it?* (1Corinthians 4:7)

Once you become born again, the Bible tells us that we are new creations in Christ Jesus. Behold old things are passed away. Our slates are fully wiped clean. You must surrender everything to the Lord, so you can walk in the new life the MOST HIGH has given you. Making Jesus Lord and Savior over your life means that you are now willing to turn the reign of your life over to him. He will now take your life and do what He wants with it. And sometimes the first thing the Lord will do is to take you back to your past so as to clean up the mess that may have occurred before really moving you forward to the divine destiny that he has for you. To fully move into your future, you have to learn how to let your past fully go. We live in a very crucial moment in the history of the world. When you turn the news on, all you see and hear is sorrow, pain, hurt and anguish. For the past three decades we have seen violence and killings, more than ever before on the face of the earth. Children killing their parents, parents killing their children. Shootings going on in stores, schools, universities, airports, theaters, and concerts. And all of these violent shootings have just one root cause- PAIN. Many of the people committing this violence blamed their attitude on the society, on their rough past, and on the fact that they felt abandoned. Many blamed other people for their current life situation. And all that comes to their mind is to hurt someone. It is my belief that the reason why all of this is happening is that these children were conceived in pain, hate and hurt. So they are born and when no care is taken they grow up, and begin to act just like their mom, dad, or other significant authority figure. And the fact is, everyone is hurt and broken from their past childhood pain, their broken marriage, the goals or vision that they procrastinated in achieving, the loss of a loved one and all kinds of emotional experiences. It becomes evident that, we have a society that is hurting and in turmoil; there is a lack of tolerance. My *reason to be* is to train and sensitize the upcoming generation. My *reason to be* is to aid them in letting go of their hurt and pain and to motivate them to work on the future and destiny that is before them. My *reason to be* is to support the upcoming generation to break cycles of hurt and pain and to become a voice for change and an expression of God's love.

A REASON TO BE

> Life without Purpose is like a body without a soul.
>
> —unknown

Author Tracey Aiken

Tracey Aiken

"All my endeavors," she says. "Are to transform how we engage with each other in healthy interpersonal and romantic relationships."

Tracey S. Aiken is shining a new light on what it means to draw strength from faith and experience. For more than 13 years, she has been a compassionate, ordained minister and women's empowerment speaker. Since 2015, she has become a published author, life group facilitator, and certified professional life coach, dedicated to working with women who have been broken through relationships.

As a result of skillful, compassionate ministry and coaching, women have been given the tools of empowerment to move their lives forward beyond inadequacy and rejection towards regaining their sense of power and purpose.

Through the pain of divorce and death, she discovered that her gift for writing would become instrumental in her healing process and a catalyst by which others would receive healing. She poured all her emotions into writing and her pen became a powerful vehicle for self-awareness, self-discovery, healing and restoration.

Tracey knows with an assurance that "There is Purpose Behind the Pen" and expresses her gratitude towards those who support her ministry. She encourages her readers that throughout life's journey, healing and wholeness is attainable when one has the courage to confront their pain. She believes we must have a conviction to accept personal responsibility for our lives and embrace our process. Though life had presented great pain, it has always presented great healing. She knew that one day, the world would have access to her life and her story. This is it.

PO Box 817, Morrisville, NC
(919) 443-9105
Tsaiken@gmail.com
www.electladychronicles.com
Facebook: 2lovebeyondu / Instagram: eladychronicles

Love Beyond Your Perspective

For There's always another perspective! What is perspective? The short definition of perspective is- *a particular attitude toward or way of regarding something; a point of view; the interrelation in which a subject or its parts are mentally viewed.* Are we willing and ready to love beyond our own perspective? Especially if it conflicts with what we believe to be the truth we have told ourselves?

I grew up in rural North Carolina with three other siblings. Honestly, we were poor and did not realize we were poor because we looked around and saw many who lived much as we did. My mother, the matriarch of our family, raised us to appreciate what we had and to not allow anyone to make us feel inferior because of it. Although my parents were never married, they remained together for 42 years, until my mother died 10 years ago from lung cancer.

Growing up as a child, I can remember birthday parties celebrated for my siblings, but for some reason, they were never celebrated in my honor. In order to understand where I fall in my sibling chain, allow me to introduce you to my siblings. My eldest brother was the high school football and baseball superstar who finenessed the crowds and was loved by everyone. As a family, we supported all his high school and most of his college events. Attendance was not optional, but mandatory. I always saw him as mom's "favorite". Second born was me, Tracey, the child who was quiet, and very reserved. The one who would shed a tear if you raised your voice at her. As a young child, I was introverted and kept mostly to myself and enjoyed writing, even in my youth. As a freshman in high school, I was not privileged to attend high school sporting events with my friends, like the other high school students. This was due to my mother's theory that the shy, quiet, introverted girl who cried at the sound of someone raising their voice was "fast" and I was not going to bring a baby into her house. Interestingly enough, I only had to be disciplined once by my parents in my life. By the end of my junior year of high school, my mother finally allowed me some privileges. Then there was my younger brother who would do anything for you. He was the child who was not afraid of anything. If he was given a directive not to do something, he saw that as an opportunity to do just the opposite. It was as if in some strange way, he found the unknown consequences intriguing. He was fun; but extremely mischievous and was frequently disciplined for his behavior. He was also the child that would help mother as she labored to maintain her garden. He and our mother, both enjoyed fishing and would often go fishing and enjoyed their time together. When he was murdered at the age of 19, needless to say, my mother was heartbroken and emotionally distraught. Lastly, there's my youngest sister, the one who required the most attention because she was the youngest and a bit spoiled. As a child, she was a daddy's girl. As she moved into her teenage years, her behavior was that of a typical teenager who rebelled against authority. As children, the difference between my personality and the personality of my siblings was that they were all extroverts. I, on the other hand, was seen; but never *heard* in the same way as my siblings. Their actions commanded the attention of our parents. I grew up internalizing my feelings of being rejected by my family. While never spoken, I often had inner thoughts that made me question if I was adopted and that was the reason for the lack of connectedness.

June 1987, was finally a reality; I was graduating high school! Since I had never felt a sense of love and belonging in our home, I had a secret excitement knowing I could finally leave my parents' household. The thought that I was an adult and could make my own decisions and command my own life was exciting! What was the most extreme thing I could do? Who would have guessed it? The quiet, shy, introverted girl had made a huge decision to enlist in the military. Surprisingly enough, when I had the conversation with my parents, they were in agreement. By November, I was heading to Basic Training. I was on my way to my heart being made happy; so I thought.

Although I was no longer in the home, my heart had an emptiness and longing for the nurturing that I had missed during my formative years. This longing for love and nurturing set into motion some unhealthy patterns that would lead to a string of broken relationships for a long period of my life. It established a pattern of focusing on what a man said, versus what his actions were. I now know this to be a similar pattern, that I had witnessed in my parents' home, throughout my childhood. This pattern involved an accepting of unacceptable behavior from a man and downplaying it in my own heart. I convinced myself that because I was strong enough to handle it, I should.

While I believe wholeheartedly, the biblical truth that marriage is honorable, my personal experience is that it has been anything but honorable for me. I was in a 14-year marriage that was pretty good for about 12 years. Then my husband decided that he would allow a mid-life crisis to lead him down a path where his choices no longer reflected the importance of putting his family first. His behavior began to exemplify a husband who placed no value on spending time with his family. He was in a dark place and his actions were both selfish and self-serving. Wherein, I was once his partner in helping to fight the battles of life, he turned to other women for comfort. His life became one with patterns, habits and cycles of partying with his friends every weekend. I can recall one day when I inquired of him- "Why are you doing these things" and he responded- "I don't care about anything or anyone at this point in my life." Those words instantly took on life and became hands, fastened around my neck, strangling the very life out of me! After 12 years, is this what the person who says he loves me, would really say to me? I was crushed and my heart was shattered into a million pieces! Shortly after this, he moved out of the home and I was forced to learn how to live my life without him. The truth is, I quickly discovered that I had merged so much of who I was into who he was, that without him, I could not recognize myself. What a journey of discovery was lying ahead.

At this time, our children were five and eleven and could not fully understand what was happening and I did not have the vocabulary, at that time, to articulate it clearly. We were all hurting. Most nights I could not sleep and would go to the kids' rooms and could hear them crying in their beds. They missed their dad and I was completely and utterly helpless to ease their pain. There are no words a parent can say to ease the pain that a child feels when their little hearts are yearning for their absent parent. All I knew to do was hug them and remind them that both dad and I loved them. Although I was angry with my husband for walking out on us, I never used my feelings and emotions as an opportunity to speak negatively about him to his children. While I did not make up lies, I did not operate in full disclosure of adult truths concerning what had happened between their dad and I. Sometimes, parents who are separating make the error of disclosing too much information to children, and either intentionally or unintentionally, leave them with a feeling of being caught in the middle.

My journey to divorce included a two-year separation; it was very painful. Within the first six months of the separation, I had thoughts of suicide as I struggled to comprehend how I could give so much of myself and end up with nothing. How could the strands of my heart be connected to a man who could cut them so easily with the scissors of infidelity. Mutual acquaintances would come to me and tell me of the things that were being said about why he left. As you can imagine, I was projected as the scapegoat and the reason he could not remain in the marriage. I also heard the unsolicited stories from acquaintances who would see him out with his mistress and would share the details with me. The agony my heart felt was overwhelming. My household was shattered! I was emotionally, spiritually and financially bankrupt! Oftentimes, it was a struggle just to figure out how I would feed my children. To date, I believe the McDonald's dollar menu was God's blessing in my life during that season. I would purchase two sandwiches, and a small fry to split between my kids and I would not eat. They were my concern through all of the turmoil. The embarrassment and pain of it all weighed heavily upon me. The question that I struggled with the most, was asking myself, "What is wrong with me." Surely there was something wrong with me if this man could walk away with no thought to our wellbeing. Maybe, I didn't cook enough; although, I did it six days out of seven. Perhaps I did not please him sexually, or as often as he desired; although that was never an issue for us. These questions consumed my thoughts daily. I felt that if I could find some reason to justify his leaving, I would be able to accept that this horrible thing had happened in my life and in the life of my children. I could experience a range of emotions within a matter of minutes; and at times, anger ruled. Those emotions would range from fear to anger; then from sadness to frustration as I worried about how I was going to pay all the bills and buy food to eat. I was as typical as any other scorned woman and contemplated how I could get even with him. If hurt people, hurt people…then I needed to get mine in. Again, all those emotions and thoughts happened within a matter of a few minutes. As I moved beyond the sixth month of the separation, my emotional stability weakened. I was unable to sleep, it was difficult to get out of bed and I lacked the energy to enjoy the things I liked or to aid in the normal daily functioning of the household.

    I recall one Saturday night; I was in the bathroom, staring at the razor blade that I held in my hand. I desperately wanted to end my life because my heart hurt so badly! I was hopeless and felt that life no longer had meaning for me. How could I ever live without this man in my life? I was in so much pain. As I stood there crying, I heard a voice that said- "Who's going to take care of your kids?" In that moment, I dropped the razor blade and called on the God that I remembered my grandmother serving! On the next day, Sunday morning, I awoke and decided to dress myself and my children and go to church. Unknowing to me, I was about to meet the *Lover of my Soul*. A Man who is unlike any other man. *God.* The preacher ministered, and I wept uncontrollably at the idea of a love that is unconditional. A love that promises to never leave or forsake me. After all, I was in the middle of feeling forsaken by love; so the preacher's message sounded both suspect and tempting. At the end of the message, there was an altar call for prayer and I found the courage to go forward for prayer. In doing so, I decided in that moment that I was broken and needed a change; a restoration. I accepted the Lord into my heart, not fully understanding the relationship and commitment at that time. My misguided perspective was that immediately, everything was going to be alright in my life. *Now,* I understand that it does not happen that way. Even then, it soon became clear that my accepting the Lord opened me up for the Lord to abide with me as he walked me through my journey of recovery and my journey of life. During this process my mood swings, insomnia and debilitation were diagnosed as being clinical depression and I was treated with prescribed medications. Finally, I was beginning to function again.

After two years of separation, and no movement or urgency from my husband to initiate divorce proceedings, I made a decision to file for divorce. Although painful, it was time for me to move on with my life. The painful truth was, he did not want a monogamous marriage with me and that was not about me; nor was it my fault. It was about him and his choices.

My perspective of love was distorted as a result of the conflicted relationship with my parents and the shattered relationship with my ex-husband. Here's what I understand today. Two years before my mother died of cancer in 2009, we reconciled our relationship. Two days before her death, she apologized for my childhood and told me that she always loved me. That as a child, she saw an inner strength in me that required less attention. She wanted me to know it was never done to hurt me. In that very moment, my heart soared and then dropped. First, I knew I had received a blessing from the Lord, hearing my mother say this before she died. Unfortunately, I realized that I had allowed a faulty perspective to steal valuable years that I could have spent building a healthy relationship with my mother; if only I had known. As an adult, I could have taken the initiative to have healed the relationship many years earlier; but I didn't. Now, I am convinced that we must not allow pride or the *victim mentality* to steal time and opportunity from us to be reconciled to those we love. Don't be afraid to put your heart out there and hold the conversations that could heal and restore relationships that are meaningful in your life. Not all relationships can be healed and that's okay. However, we will not know unless we try.

Somehow, with the separation and divorce from my husband, pain shaped my perspective, convincing me that I was responsible for his infidelity. Absolutely not! While I was 100% monogamous, I accept that I was not without faults. However, counseling helped me to understand that I was not responsible for the actions of another person. So, what is my reason to be? The word *BE* means ***to exist as***!

PURPOSE REFLECTIONS:

- My Reason to Be – Is *Love* – I have received the greatest Love; His Love.

- The inability and unwillingness to hear another's perspective ruins relationships.

- An intentional healing process restores us and makes it possible to *Love Beyond* our faulty perspective.

- We must accept that adults make adult decisions and sometimes those decisions are selfish and hurt us in the process. In essence, the individual is trying to satisfy their own desires. As a result, we become casualties in the war of their spirit and their soul.

- There is a *Divine* empowerment of *Grace* that enables us to *Love Beyond* our faulty perspective, making it possible and probable.

For more on healing from relational hurt, follow me in my private Facebook group: Love Beyond: An Open Heart is a Willing Heart.

A REASON TO BE

Don't be pushed around by your fears, but rather led by your Purpose!

Author Regal Cameron

Regal Cameron

As a Certified Life Coach, Speaker and Published Author Regal T. Cameron is living proof that no matter what happens in life, she still comes out on top! She is known as Raw & Real Regal. In her desire to help others, she created *Regal Life Academy* to serve her tribe with life changing self-help and self-development tools needed to build self-esteem, self-love and confidence. Regal focuses on those individuals that desire to make real change in their life.

At the age of five, Regal experienced child sexual abuse, at the hands of her babysitter's daughter. The daughter was much older than Regal and threaten to beat her up, if she told. At ten, Regal faced another abuse incident, at the hands of her mother's boyfriend. When Regal built up the courage to share her abuse with her mother, her mother's response was to call her a "liar". The molestation continued for a year until the boyfriend was caught, by Regal's mother, and thrown out of the house. Regal also faced mental abuse, at the hands of her mother, and suffered a rape, from an ex fiancé, while serving in the military. Regal uses her past abuse to build and bless others. It is her passion to help others come to terms with past hurts, by teaching them the power of forgiveness and breaking their brokenness. Regal desires to empower women to face their fears, let go of their anger, and push past their pain.

Regal is a veteran of the US Armed Forces, where she served over five years. She also served as a Federal Civil Servant for ten years. Regal received an Associate Degree in Liberal Arts from Saint Leo's University and a Bachelor's Degree in Business Administration, with a Concentration in Management from Strayer University; where she graduated Magna Cum Laude.

Regal has appeared on several platforms. She has served as a guest speaker for She Is You Facebook Group, She's Broken Telesummit, SAW Ambassador Facebook Group, The Strength of Authentic Women SAW Telesummit and the Leader's Circle Radio Show. Regal is the author of *Divine Intervention, A Daily Devotional Inspired by the Holy Spirit* and *I Choose Me: The Real Women's Guide of How to Get Over It For Real*, to be publish in September 2019.

Regal is the owner of RTC Destiny and Regal Life Academy, where she serves as a Speaker and Life Coach. Her mission is to help women, "Heal the child within so the adult can live."

Journey to Purpose

As I sat in my bedroom, staring at the pink walls, my mind wondered; "what am I supposed to be? What do I want to do when I grow up? Do I want to be a writer? Or, should I be a singer? Or, maybe a hairdresser? What the heck am I going to do with my life?" I thought to myself. At the age of twelve, I had no idea of truly who or what I wanted to be. For a while, I tried to write poetry but I would get painful headaches. So, I let go of that idea for a while. I did a couple things growing up; trying to find my gifts. Throughout elementary and Junior High, I was in choir at school. I added track, to the equation, in junior high school.

It was during the 8th grade talent show that my gifting began to shine. I decided to audition for the talent contest with my rendition of a Sukiyaki song, *A Taste of Honey*. This was a popular 1980's group. I was so excited that I made the cut!!! My Aunt Terri helped me with my outfit. She made me a short, satin, off-white mini skirt with a royal blue top, sash, and a headband. I was too cute! I practiced every day until the show. I was so nervous to sing in front of people, but I did it anyway. I loved singing then and I was pretty good at it, if I must say so myself. Finally, the big day came. It was a Friday. All the contestants were backstage as the stage director instructed us on how the show was going to work. This was the first time I saw my competition... My nerves got worse as I realized that I was going up against Ed Fleming, the class "Super Talent". Everyone knew he was going to mwin first place, because he was known for his voice and his Michael Jackson moves. I had a crush on him, like all the girls. The show started and contestants began to perform, gathering a nice applause. Then Ed went up to sing a Michael Jackson song, I can't remember which one, but I know he got a resounding applause. Then it was my turn. I was so nervous!!! I sang over the track because, back then, I didn't know about instrumental music. I did it; sang in front of a live audience!!! I was so proud myself. A few more students performed after me. Then, it was time to announce the WINNERS! The first and second place winners were announced. I was neither; I just knew that I hadn't won. So, I closed my eyes and prayed, waiting for the third-place winner's named to be called. The announcer began, "The third-place winner iiiisssss Regal Cameron!!!" IT WAS ME!!! I opened my eyes, screaming, "YES, YES, YES, I WON!!!" I ran right by Ed Fleming, on to the stage, to collect my prize of $20!!! At that moment, I just knew I would have a career as a singer. I also won other singing competitions and received a superior rating, singing acapella at choir nationals, in Atlanta, Georgia. I just knew I was meant to sing, until my confidence was shattered by tight competition. My self-esteem was not that strong, as a teenager.

As I got a little older, my interest changed. I decided to become a hairdresser. My Mom was a hairdresser, when I was a little girl. She taught me how to do my hair and, I must say, I was pretty dog-gone good at doing hair. I could curl my entire head without a mirror, never burning myself. I could cut, perm, and style my hair all by myself. I still can do it, to this day. I had a conversation with my Uncle Ted, and he talked me out of being a hairdresser. In so many words, he said there were enough hairdressers in our family, and I should do something different. I listened and started to look for other options.

I graduated high school and went off to Polk Community College. I met with my guidance counselor to decide what my major would be. I wanted to go into business; not sure what business I was going to do, but I knew that I wanted to be an entrepreneur. Wrong answer, according to my counselor. She said that too many people were going into business and that I should find something else to do. I felt defeated, because for once, I was sure about what I wanted, even though I didn't have a specific business in mind. I knew I wanted to be my own boss. Years later, I regretted not listening to my first instinct. I was young and looking for guidance. Unfortunately, my counselor gave me the wrong guidance.

My first major in college was Physical Education. I thought it would be easy and a way to earn a living. That was a short-lived major choice. I realized, as I took classes, that I had no passion for physical education. That ended and I just focused on getting my core classes completed, to pursue a Liberal Arts degree. Next thing I knew I was joining the Army I was five classes away from achieving my Associate Degree in Liberal Arts. You see, the closer I got to graduation, the more my Mother asked for money. I was working, to save money for school and preparing to transfer to Fort Valley State University in Georgia. The closer my departure date got, the more my Mom needed me to help with the household expenses. I felt trapped. I was trying to make a life for myself only to be held back because my mother did not want to take on the role of being grown and taking care of herself.

I had been helping my Mom for years and was tired of doing for her and needed to do for myself. Therefore, I made the decision to leave and go into the Army. From the time I enlisted, it took me two weeks to leave my Mom's house. This was the best decision I ever made for my life. I finally took complete control of my life. I chose ME for the first time in my life. For the first time, I did not consult anyone or listen to anyone's suggestions or concerns. I just LEAPED!!!

I served in the Army from May of 1991 to November of 1997. During that time, I finished my Associate Degree in Liberal Arts and started on my path to working on my Business Degree, following my first instinct. During my military years, I went through ups and downs learning myself and figuring out life. Personally, I went through my first spiritual awakening. I found God. I joined a church and got involved with ministry. I sang in the choir, worked in the prison, hospitality, and singles ministries, just to name a few. Eventually, I realized I had my own personal ministry and spiritual gifts that needed to be developed; thus, I started working towards getting my ministerial license. Internal church issues became a distraction, causing me to stop pursuing my license. I did not agree with the church's way of doing things. I would have questions about why things were done a particular way. When I shared my opinions, I was dismissively told not to worry about it and just finish the class. Consequently, I did my own research, on the questions that I had, which revealed a very narrow way of thinking within my church. I also experienced a lot of church hurt. I realized that **some** of these Christians were the meanest, most disrespectful and hateful people that I had ever met. After all of my negative experiences within my church, I felt discouraged and left. I was desperately searching for *My Reason To Be*.

After my honorable discharge from the military, in November 1997, I decided to move to Savannah, Georgia. I worked at CVS Pharmacy as a pharmacy technician and re-enrolled in school to complete my degree. That was short lived, because I listened to my current boyfriend, at the time. He persuaded me to move back home, to Florida, for him. LADIES, NEVER MOVE FOR A MAN!!! I digress, back to the story at hand. I transferred my job and moved into a boarding house. YES, a boarding house. I was so lost spiritually, physically, and mentally. My life was in shambles, trying to pick up the pieces of a series of bad decisions. This was the beginning of my second spiritual awakening. I was truly finding myself and identifying who were my real friends (these were very few), and committed family members (many had turned their backs on me). I had to put on my "Big-Girl Panties" and grow up. I had to dig really deep and find the woman I was meant to be. Pulling myself up, by my bootstraps, was one of the hardest things I have ever had to do. My life literally depended on it. Eventually, life started to come together and searching for *My Reason To Be* returned.

During the summer of 1999, I was sitting in a Subway eating lunch and reading my journal of poetry. This was my way of writing down my feelings and experiences of life. As I read my words, I realized that I was broken, hurt, angry, negative, and miserable. I was that stereotypical; "Angry Black Woman". I was actually the poster girl for the "Angry Black Woman!" You see, when you never address your "ish", it lives in your present and eats away at your future, because you never dealt with your past. This was the first time, in my life, that I realized I needed mental help and needed to do some self-work. At that time, I didn't even know it was called "personal development" (third spiritual awakening), but I knew I needed to do something. The journey began with going to the book store and getting self-help books on forgiveness and self-love. I created a forgiveness exercise and I began to look in the mirror and say, "I forgive Mama for _____." I would say it over and over and over again until I did not feel the pain associated with the incident. I did this with every person I needed to forgive in my life. This exercise helped me let go of the brokenness, hurt, angry, negative feelings and brought me joy. Some things fell right off and others took time, depending on the severity of the hurt.

You may be asking, how is this going to help me get to my Reason to Be? When you are searching for purpose there is a journey you go on to find self. Purpose cannot come without first learning who you are. All of this put me on the path of writing, which is part of my purpose. I took that journal and turned it into my first book, *Divine Intervention, A Daily Devotional Inspired By The Holy Spirit*. I wrote publishing houses, sending in my transcript, only to be told, "thank you, but no thank you." It was very discouraging that no one wanted to publish my poetry. I put the book down, thinking maybe I'm not a writer and continued to work on me.

Fast forward to 2015. After years of working on myself, I finally reached a point in my healing that I could speak openly about my past abuses and experiences. I found myself looking for purpose. I wanted to go into business for myself. I started a side hustle; promoting and selling Traci Lynn Jewelry. This was the beginning of my entrepreneurial journey. Becoming a Traci Lynn Consultant changed my life!!! Traci Lynn, the owner and founder, taught me about multiple streams of income and going after your dreams. I used Traci Lynn Jewelry to do that. While training and growing as an entrepreneur, I met a consultant that connected me to my first business coach. She taught me how to publish books. YES!!!! I self-published my first book, *Divine Intervention, A Daily Devotional Inspired By The Holy Spirit*. Delayed not denied!!! My purpose was now in print. After learning how to publish my book, I thought I was to become a publisher. Wrong!!! As the journey continued, I realized God had just put me in the path of someone who could help me accomplish what needed to be done. God allowed me to accomplish my desire to write and have a published book. In publishing my book, my pain gave purpose to my life. I was telling my stories to help people deal with their pains, hurts, anger, and brokenness. I knew then that I had to go deeper.

Deeper meant I needed to find a way to talk about my hard truth. I had to talk about the molestation, the rape, and the mental abuse. I had to talk about the core hard truth people don't want to speak about. This was hard to come to terms with because telling my core hard truth left me naked for all to see. It took me another two and a half years to get to a point that I could talk about my core hard truth with transparency. I had to get comfortable with all my "ish"; the good, the bad, and the ugly. I took speaking classes, so that I could get comfortable speaking in front of people. Then, I started speaking via social media. I spoke on videos and lives on my Facebook and Instagram, but I knew that I had to go deeper. Deeper meant I had to find the tools to coach people through their issues and get to a resolve in a positive way.

I started searching for coaching programs and found P4 Coaching Institute. P4 Coaching Institute gave me the foundational tools to build programs that help people to *Live their Best Life*. I learned how to help people break the cycle of brokenness through my program; *Review – Reflect – Connect.* First, I walk clients through *Reviewing* their life, then *Reflecting* over their life's personal relationships and finally, *Connecting* to who they want to be. Through this process, I show them *How To Get Over It For Real, Steps To Forgiveness,* and how to *Activate Their Confidence Frequen*cy. All these programs are in my book, "*I Choose Me, The Real Woman's Guide to Getting Over It For Real.*" I now realize that everything I went through, the trainings I took, programs I created and the books I have written, brought me to the point of finding my purpose. In being transparent and coaching and helping others, I now have *A Reason To Be.*

A REASON TO BE

Follow your passion and it will lead you to your purpose!

Author Marlene Fuller

Marlene Fuller

Marlene was born and raised in Chicago, Illinois and later relocated to Vicksburg, Mississippi. During her childhood, she survived abandonment from her biological mother that resulted in years of struggling with the spirit of rejection. As a result of her brokenness and pain she has a heartfelt passion for ministering to women suffering from abandonment and rejection. As a young adult, Marlene enlisted in the United States Air Force where she served for ten years. She completed her military career at Seymour Johnson AFB, Goldsboro, NC.

Marlene answered the call to preach the gospel in October 2001 and was ordained through North West B Conference of the United American Free Will Baptist Denomination in November 2006. She holds a Bachelor degree from Christian Bible College & Seminary in Theological Studies and a Certificate in Church Leadership from Bear Creek Missionary Baptist Association. Marlene has a Bachelor of Arts degree in Organizational Administration with a concentration in Organizational Development and a Bachelor of Science in Religious Studies, from NC Wesleyan College. She graduated Magna Cum Laude.

Marlene is as an associate minister at Impact Church-Goldsboro, located in Goldsboro, NC under the leadership of Apostles Edwin & Catherine Newsome. She has served as the director of the "Women of Destiny Ministry. Previously" She is happily married to Minister Robert E. Fuller Jr. and they have been blessed with a beautiful daughter. They reside in Lagrange, NC.

Marlene truly believes that "All things work together for good" her life is a testimony of this. Along with her husband they are the founders of Fuller Life Ministries, Where their motto is "You Can Have a Fuller Life in Christ" She believes that the level of your anointing is directly related to the level of pain you have experienced.

Your Setbacks Are Just Setups

I survived to live another day to help another person. At an early age, my life was targeted by the enemy. I believe Satan tried to destroy me from the onset of my birth in an effort to stop the future plans and purposes that God has for me. God's plans are designed to ultimately affect others and bring deliverance and healing to those who have had similar experiences as I did.

Out of four siblings I was the only one who mainly experienced extreme abuse. From the age of eight into adulthood there was mental and physical abuse at the hands of those who were supposed to love and protect me. I experienced fear of my mom and as an adult, rejection from a man who I thought loved me. There were many, many other traumatic incidents that occurred in the years in between. I also experienced many failed relationships, when I just wanted to experience real love. It sent me on a path of looking for love in all the wrong places. The search for love almost destroyed my life on so many levels!

I have come to realize, which also allows me to encourage other women, that the realization of the trauma must be exposed. The pain from the trauma will resurface if not spiritually and emotionally dealt with. However, as I myself am a witness, with God's intervention and the help of others, your healing can come forth.

I have been healed from the fear that came with the abandonment of my mother who suffered from a mental illness. She would often try to harm us as children; me in particular. The effect of being afraid of the very person who is supposed to love you was debilitating. My siblings and I, often had to be removed from her supervision, for our own protection. The trauma of seeing your own mother, in such a rage, threatening you with a knife and then being carried off in a straightjacket, leaves quite a devastating effect on a child. This became a regular thing, as my mother was in and out of mental hospitals throughout my childhood; until one day she just never returned home. I never connected with my mother because she showed little interest in any of her children, due to her illness. She would talk to herself and would say she heard voices. This was frightening and very traumatic for me as a child.

These traumatic experiences with my mother, led me into so much more abuse and mental bondage. Becoming separated from my mom, now meant my father had to raise us. Unfortunately, my siblings and I received much of my father's anger and disappointment with the life that was now dealt to him. Daily, I received a reminder of his disappointment, in the form of physical beatings and verbal abuse. The verbal abuse was paralyzing. I was called *stupid* every day, and my entire childhood was rooted in fear. My grandfather, who had Alzheimer's, lived with us. This became an additional stressor for me because often on weekends, we were left alone with him while my dad was out with his female friends.

Eventually, the family was split up and my oldest sister and I moved to live with our grandparents and aunt. Even though my grandmother and aunt showed me much love and took great care of me, the spirit of rejection had already fallen hard on me and had attacked my self-esteem. The seeds of non-acceptance had taken root. The feelings of inadequacy followed me even into adulthood where I made life- altering mistakes.

However, I thank God for having an aunt who showed me the love of Jesus through her life and lifestyle. I didn't fully understand it then, but having God in my life was going to rescue me. I attended church with her each time she went. I enjoyed seeing her shout and praise the Lord. Later in life when I accepted Jesus as my Lord and Savior, I allowed God to heal my brokenness. There are many forms of brokenness in life; but as a little girl not having the love and nurturing of a mother was devastating and it almost destroyed me!

With the death of my grandmother came yet another traumatic experience. The loss of someone who really cared was even harder on me than the separation of my mother. My grandmother had shown me love and nurtured me; as I was a sickly child and always needed physical attention as well as emotional care. When she died, I was still very young and struggling to understand it all.

After my grandmother's death, my dad moved all my siblings and me to his hometown in Mississippi. My love for God stayed with me even though I was not with my aunt anymore. I began attending an apostolic church with a friend and accepted the Lord as my Savior at the age of seventeen. The people from the church were kind and giving. They would pick me up for church services and choir rehearsal. However, this did not sit well with my dad. I believe the thought of me going to church and other people helping me, angered him. So, as a result he would punish me with a belt; but the whippings didn't stop me. I went anyway, and just dealt with the punishment. God was my lifeline in this horrendous situation. The saints at the church would give me money as they shook my hand. God was taking care of my siblings and me, even when we didn't understand it all. With the money that was provided, I was able to buy our food. Often, my dad would refuse to buy food. Many nights my siblings and I went hungry and dirty because the refrigerator was empty and the water bill was not paid.

With God's help, I made it through those traumatic years and was able to graduate high school and then attend college. I was hopeful and wanted to pursue a degree in Nursing. However, I was unable to complete college because I lacked financial support from my family. So, I tried working various jobs but realized that I needed and wanted more out of life. In 1987, I joined the United States Air Force, where I served for ten years as an Aircraft Maintenance Data Analyst. However, traumatic situations continued to follow me. The past abuse and lack of a father's love, continually made me feel unworthy of the love of a good man. I really had no clue what genuine love looked like. So, again the abuse continued. While in the United States Air Force I spent seven years in a mentally abusive relationship with a man who never loved me. As a result of the stress of the abusive relationship, I experienced a miscarriage that left me unable to have biological children. This threw me into a state of depression and became too much for me to bear. I wanted to be a mother so badly. I felt that I had so much love and affection to give. I wanted to give a child something I never had; which was love.

Despite it all, God has made my life a testimony that broken crayons still color. Yes! Broken crayons still color! Regardless of what I've been through, I can still love and want to be loved because I know a God who *is* love. To God be the glory! As all things work together for the good of them that love the lord! Each traumatic experience seemed to be just a necessary part of my journey until the day I was set free by Jesus Christ. I soon realized, God had not called me to a life of misery but to a life of victory and joy! Around 1997, while in the Air Force, stationed at Seymour Johnson Air Force Base, Goldsboro, North Carolina, I met a young lady who invited me to her church. It was there, at Greater Guiding Star United Holy Church, that I re-dedicated my life to Christ; that day my life changed forever. The pastor preached a sermon entitled, "When Your Salt has Lost its Savor". That day I sat at the back of the church, but the Lord drew me to the altar. Prior to this, I knew that I needed to come back to my first love; I just really didn't know how. In my heart, one thing that I wanted was to *kneel* before God. Guess what? The pastor asked everyone at the altar to *kneel*! This was indeed, my confirmation that God loved me unconditionally. Despite what happened previously, God was able to bring me out and deliver me into His marvelous light. He opened the gate that kept me bound, and since then, I have come to work through and overcome some of life's greatest setbacks; fear, shame and anxiety.

I had the awesome opportunity at a previous ministry to oversee a women's ministry that focused on women who have gone through traumatic situations. I believe I have become a lighthouse in dark places for children and women; to help them see that true healing comes when we release the shame and acknowledge the trauma. I guide them to couple this with seeking the word of God and seeking professional help.

I have become a conduit for women in bad marriages and for children growing up in a troubled environment. Through my understanding and experience, I am able to bring them a message of hope. My message is to not be discouraged with all that has happened in your life but to understand you can be set free and God has a plan and purpose for your life.

My true transformation began once I returned back to God. As my relationship with my heavenly Father developed, I began to see the broken places in my life and recognize my need for healing. Through the word of God, I began to see how God uses different adversities to get people to their expected end. I began to acknowledge the love that God has for us. He did not neglect or forsake me during those traumatic years but was there with a purpose and plan and one of the plans was for me to be a blessing to others.

My life was a clear example that God had a purpose for me even before I was born. On October 21, 2001, I preached my initial sermon entitled, "It's Working For My Good" (Romans 8:28/ Romans 8:18 & Genesis 50:19-20). In November, 2006 I was ordained at the United American Free Will Baptist Headquarters, Kinston, North Carolina. My aunt and I would have many conversations on the phone about the Lord, my ministry, and how she was so very proud of me. Our conversations always ended with her telling me to- "STAY WITH GOD". In one of our conversations, she told me that she wanted me to deliver her eulogy. I was shocked and troubled. This was something that I didn't want to discuss. She made me promise that I would honor her request. Then she gave me specific instructions how she wanted things to go. To make me laugh, she said that she wasn't going anywhere; she was going to live to be 100 years old! This conversation happened around September or October, 2008. On November 30, 2008, I received a call that my aunt had passed during the night in her apartment. My heart literally dropped and so did I, to the floor. My

Pillar, my Mother, my Prayer Warrior was gone. Another terrific blow! This one really hurt me to my core. The one person left in my life that I knew for sure loved me was gone! Without God during this time, I could never have survived this one. It took all of the *Strength of God* to carry me through.

I traveled from North Carolina to Chicago, Illinois, with my Pastor and completed what my aunt had asked me to do. On December 4, 2008, I eulogized my Aunt/Mother; the sermon was entitled- "Stay with God" (Romans 8:35-39). The Lord carried me through. To have me eulogize my aunt, was definitely an honor for me and my family. The service was held at Greater Harvest Missionary Baptist Church; the very same church that I attended with my aunt as a child. Oh, the memories! This had come full circle. Who would have ever thought this little girl that slept on the pews while service was going on would be standing in the pulpit declaring the word of God. Just like I ministered at my initial sermon- "IT'S WORKING FOR MY GOOD!" God has truly had a plan and a purpose for my life. My prayer is that God will continue to be glorified through my life. I understand even the more, that I had to be broken so that the love and oil of God could be poured out. I'm excited about my future in the kingdom!

On July 23, 2011 I married my best friend, Robert Earl Fuller Jr, a man chosen by God just for me. He is my best friend, lover, cheerleader, chef and so much more, and I'm a mother to a beautiful step-daughter whom I love dearly. My life is truly a testimony that God will allow everything that you have been through to be a blessing to others. In addition, He will bless you abundantly; giving you double for your trouble!

Finally, we overcome setbacks best, when we keep looking ahead instead of behind. Make no mistake, this response to setbacks is not typical. It will go against your instincts. But if you desire to make progress in your spiritual life, you'll have to leave the old behind. In the difficult times, when your enemies seem to have gotten the best of the situation, just trust God! Look at the Gospels of Jesus Christ. His life didn't end when people or the enemy wanted it to. God used all of the setbacks for the greatest come back. Jesus suffered, died and was buried ...the good news is that he got up! It's the exact same principle in life. When people treat you unfairly, don't lose focus and most of all, don't quit. Always remember that the very things that have hurt you will thrust you to the next level in your walk with the Lord. The Lord desires to bring you higher in every area, and He wants the best for your life. God desires to guide you to the pathway of the destiny he has designed just for you! Your SETBACK is just a setup!

You'll have to trust God with your failures and defeats. Just know that he has it all in control. You can and will overcome every adversity life brings to you! I thank everyone who played a part in my life; the good, the bad and the ugly. I definitely wouldn't be the woman of God that I have become without them all. All of the trauma, verbal abuse, fear, anxiety, abandonment and broken promises could have,- should have destroyed me ...but God said, no! *You are not a victim but a victor.* "And Joseph said unto them, fear not: for am I in the place of God? But as for you, ye thought evil against me; but God meant it unto good, to bring to pass, as it is this day, to save much people alive" (Genesis 50:19-20).

"It don't matter what you tried to do, you couldn't destroy me! I'm still standing. I'm still strong! And I always will be "

- Antwone Fisher Story, 2002.

I survived...To live another day...To help another person!

Minister and Author- Marlene P. Fuller

A REASON TO BE

God put people in your life on purpose, so that you can be a blessing to them!

Author Erica Perry Green

Erica Perry Green

Erica Perry Green is a woman who has risen against great odds to find her *reason to be*! With an intense passion and desire to see everyone win, Erica focused her career on leading, coaching and mentoring sales professionals in the corporate space. Erica has held managerial and executive level positions in both pharmaceutical companies and educational firms. Managing multi-million dollar accounts and sales professionals across six states, Erica currently serves as a Regional Executive Director of Healthcare. Erica has focused her twenty-year career in sales, marketing and training.

While rising through the ranks in Corporate America, Erica had a strong desire to own her own business and create a legacy that would out-live her. For the last six years, Erica has been successful in various business and marketing endeavors; including launching SHERO Publishing Company, focused on helping women to Unleash their inner SHERO and share their stories with the world. Erica is also a three-time author herself; publishing her book, *Unleash Your SHERO* and sharing her literary work as a co-author in both *Love Pack* and *Wake, Pray, Slay*. Erica also founded Green Business Consulting Firm, supporting entrepreneurs to grow, scale, and market their business. Erica serves as an ICF Certified Business & Life Coach, supporting business owners to maximize their success.

As a skilled entrepreneur, Erica has traveled the world, training and assisting new business owners in growing and developing their brand. Erica is passionate about mentoring and coaching entrepreneurs on the concept of multiple streams of income. Erica has also ascended to top ranks in two global businesses; creating networks of thousands of business partners. As a master sales trainer and marketer, Erica is also partnered with Lipsynk Cosmetics, serving as their Global Sales & Marketing Director for the entire Ambassador Sales Team; expanding the company globally.

With an intense passion for giving back, Erica founded Sisters Lifting Sisters, a nonprofit focused on supporting women and children at risk, including those facing hunger issues, single mothers, domestic violence survivors, women facing homelessness, and women facing health issues. To date, SLS Nonprofit has supported over 6,000 women and children through annual food and clothing pantries, GIRLS 2 WOMEN Empowerment events, backpack drives and hosting an annual Christmas brunch and gift giveback for women and their families in residential rehabilitation facilities in Wake and Orange County.

Throughout all of her philanthropic endeavors, family remains first! Erica enjoys traveling the world and spending time with her loving husband and best friend of sixteen years, Jonathan Green, and daughter, Camryn. Following in her mother's footsteps, Camryn became a CEO at the age of 8. She is now a sophomore in high school. Erica works hard to ensure that Camryn is raised, understanding that she must utilize her gifts and talents to empower others and above all else, serve her community. She truly is one of Erica's *reasons to be*!

Connect with Erica Perry Green:
Business Coaching: ericaperrygreen.com
Publishing: sheropublishing.com
Facebook: @ericaperrygreen
Instagram: @ericapgreen
ericaperrygreen@gmail.com
(919) 522-8195

Not My Plan, But HIS!

FINALLY, I had made it! I was now a graduate from one of the most prestigious universities in the country, The University of North Carolina at Chapel Hill with one of the most sought-after degrees. I had the esteemed pleasure of being accepted into UNC's Gillings School of Public Health, the number two School of Public Health in the country (U.S. News). I was now working as a Pharmaceutical Rep; a hospital gladiator in a suit!

I always had very detailed goals. I wanted to graduate by 21, start working in Corporate America, wearing designer suits, by 25 and achieve a six-figure salary by 30. I was well on my way to crushing all my goals well before my deadlines. I felt as though I must definitely be on the path to my purpose. I was getting it done, but I would soon realize that there was too much "I" and not enough "HIM."

Thankfully, well before I had the job or degree, I already had "The Man". My Prince Charming showed up at a 4-H camp the summer before my freshman year in high school. Yes, I met my husband before I could drive a car! We were close friends through my high school journey and solidified our relationship, during our senior year, attending each other's proms and committing to be exclusive. After high school graduation, we both attended college within a 30-minute drive from each other; I at UNC and my soon-to-be hubby, at North Carolina State University. I honestly believe that not attending the same college truly strengthened and saved our relationship, throughout our college years! I would later realize that God was giving me a earthly protector, as the storms I faced were meant to crush and kill me.

As I sailed through my twenties, life was a dream. I was moving forward in my career, meeting influential people in my corporate company and making a name for myself, within my North Carolina territory. It took a lot for me, a young black woman, to win over doctors in rural Eastern North Carolina. When I graduated, my position placed me in a place of authority, knowing more than even the physicians, on the antibiotics and pain medications that they were prescribing. I quickly realized that having the knowledge did not garner you their respect. It was a shell-shock for me to move from Chapel Hill, North Carolina back to rural Greenville, North Carolina for my sales position. I faced racism on a level that I had never experienced it before.

Many of the local physicians were Caucasian and not used to seeing strong, educated African-American women enter their offices, wheeling their samples. I would receive many inappropriate questions, from, "How old are you, Gal?" "How did you get this job?" "Where did you graduate?" "Where's my old rep?" and many more, too insane to even account. I faced the stares, the eye rolls, the receptionists whispering, the long wait times, cancelled appointments and denials daily. Often, I would walk boldly back to my company car, close the door and drive out of their office parking, only to pull over and let the tears roll. I knew that things would be challenging, but at times, this was too much to bear.

My managers had million-dollar goals for my territory and wouldn't understand that doctors denied me access, due to the color of my skin and the intimidation of what I represented. I knew that regardless of what "they" did to me, I had a job to do, and I would do it with excellence. I thought back on all the times that my mother had unknowingly prepared me for these very days. I can remember the fancy restaurants and hotels that she would take me and my sister to. I would sit at the table and feel all the people starring at us, as if to say, "What are these black people doing in here?" My mother, sensing the fear on my face, would always say, "Sit up tall and be confident! You bring beautiful COLOR to this room." Those words seeped into my soul, like a shield of pride and worth.

Those words got me through so many hard days at the beginning of my career. From the overt racism that I faced in the doctor's offices, to winning accounts and having the credit stolen by older, white male colleagues, I learned the hard truths about what it takes to be a *Gladiator in Corporate America*. It is a cutthroat environment and that was so hard for me to handle. I had a hard time playing *their* game, because for all the company cars, bonuses and big checks, there was something inside of me what was unsettled.

It was hard for me to stomach the fact that a lot of the drugs that created the billions in pharmaceutical wealth were simply "masking symptoms" and not getting to the root of health conditions. I had problems selling the drugs for Restless Leg or Heartburn, for I knew that they came with a high price tag and no true healing diagnosis, but I did have the pleasure of selling a life-saving antibiotic and I thrived with that drug! I won over million-dollar hospital pharmacy accounts and successfully sold this drug throughout my state. Looking back, I now realize that I was so successful with that particular drug, out of the suit of drugs that I sold, because I could get behind it's worth. You see, this drug was a hospital-strength drug, used to fight the worst of the worst infections. I knew that it was needed for life-saving treatments. I witnessed patients come back from severe illness because of this drug. I had passion in selling it because it had such value. Later in my own life, a similar antibiotic saved my infected heart. My success came with selling what I knew was worthy and valuable to others. I would even visit local pharmacies, sharing drug discount cards and savings options with the pharmacists, to help their customers get these drugs cheaply. I knew the way around the system, what to ask for and how to get overage and I wasn't afraid to share it. Even at the beginning of my career, my purpose was calling on me to serve and protect the rights of others. I wanted to give and share something that was life changing, life healing. My purpose was pushing me towards that which benefited the community versus that which simply lined pharma's pockets.

As I entered my thirties, my purpose kept pulling on me. I have always had a gift for training, connecting with others and advocating for people. My career shifted and I found myself working at Duke Hospital as a Physician Technology Trainer. I was now training physicians on how to run their new electronic medical records systems. Throughout my eight-month training assignment, all Duke hospital physicians had to complete my training and testing to maintain their positions. As I stood at the front of my classrooms, looking out at all the physicians, and as I followed them through the hospital floors as they sought my guidance and expertise to input their patient orders, I was reminded of those days that some of these same doctors used to shut me out and ignore me, now they needed me to do their jobs! Your see, GOD will make your enemies your footstool. God placed me in a place of power over the very people who denied me access. My purpose was bigger than their denial!

In those days, I realized that training and coaching were two of my God-given gifts. I went on to become a Regional Executive Manager of an education firm; coaching, training and mentoring sales professionals in six states, but I still heard GOD saying, "Take your gifts and talents to the marketplace." I have always known that I had a marketplace ministry inside of me. That is why I started my nonprofit, but GOD wanted more. I launched my business coaching firm, to inspire others to become entrepreneurs and teamed up with my girlfriend to launch a direct sales team from her successful cosmetics and lipstick line, Lipsynk Cosmetics. Over the last year, I have mentored and coached over one thousand women through the LipSynk Ambassador Program, serving as their Global Sales and Marketing Director. Pouring into these women daily, has been such a joy; it is so much bigger than LIPSTICK! I also wanted to help women, who have been through extraordinary life journeys, share their stories, so I launched SHERO Publishing, where I help women *Unleash Their SHERO*. It has been my honor to work with over 60 authors as they birth their literary works.

As I look back over my life, I can recall that great college plan and how everything was falling into place, until GOD stepped in and shook it all up. You see, our plans are not God's plans. Sometimes God has to strip you, expose you, and put you through great hurts, pains and challenges to push you towards your purpose. God broke me to make me GREATER. Everything that I have been through brought me to this day, where I can truly say that I am walking in my full and greatest potential, full of internal JOY, humbled by all that HE has done and grateful for EVERYTHING! It was all required to get me to this point, for me to find my *reason to be*!

PURPOSE REFLECTIONS:

- **Expect Obstacles, Setbacks & Opposition!**
  The road to purpose is never easy! The obstacles and setbacks are required to strengthen and prepare you to step into what God has for you. Don't fight them but recognize their worth.

- **The road to your purpose will not be a straight one!**
  Our thoughts are not God's thoughts and our ways are not HIS ways. Your journey to your purpose will have many twists and turns and ups and downs. The very things that you think are pushing you in the wrong direction might actually be propelling you forward. No matter what comes your way, keep pressing forward!

- **Stepping into your purpose requires you to let go of your FEAR.** Faith and fear can't coexist. If you want to live an authentic life, walking in your purpose, you must be FEARLESS. You must be willing to do what you must to accomplish God's mandate for your life. Walking in your purpose requires you to step out of your comfort zone and stretch!

- **Pray and God will reveal.**
  Pray for purpose and God will draw those to you to help support you in rising towards it.

Author Sandra Hardy

Sandra Hardy

Sandra Hardy is a native of Brooklyn, New York and currently resides in Raleigh, North Carolina. She graduated from Dunn High School in Dunn, North Carolina. She attended Strayer University and earned a Bachelor of Business Administration and a Master of Business Administration (MBA) both with a concentration in Human Resources Management. She currently works for the Federal Government.

Sandra is an Army Veteran with active duty and National Guard service. Her desire to help women, especially military women to advance to their full potential in life and career, lead to the development of her company- Bootz To Heelz. As the CEO and Founder, she uses her life coaching and personal branding experience to help women navigate the complexities of life by showing them how to strategize, plan and implement long and short term goals and opportunities.

Her entrepreneurial skills expanded into owning a Paparazzi Accessories business, BZ2HZ Jewel House Boutique, Mary Kay Independent Consultant business, and becoming an ambassador in Lip Synk Cosmetics. Sandra believes in providing everything a woman needs to create a powerful outer image, as she helps her build an empowering inner image. She is also an empowerment speaker and a co-author of the book, *The Purposed Woman 365 Day Devotional*.

Sandra is a single parent to a son, Marcus N. Hardy-Bannerman.

From Molestation to Purpose

You cannot talk about the end of the journey without first discussing the beginning. When people hear I am from Brooklyn, New York, their first thoughts are- ghettos, projects, and food stamps. Especially when I tell them I was raised by a single-mom. So let me begin by dispelling the myths; I actually lived in apartment buildings; normally about four apartments to a building. The area was nice; there were kids to play with and the neighbors actually cared. This part of my life was not where my tests and trials began in my life. My trials came from a mother who trusted her family to love her child, despite the fact they could not love her. My mother had a very tenuous relationship with her mother and siblings. She ran away from Selma, Alabama to Brooklyn, New York at the age of 16 for a new life; escaping the drudgery of farming and taking care of her younger siblings. I truly can understand her leaving; my grandmother was mean and evil.

    I started staying with my grandmother at a very young age; the exact age I cannot remember, because I tried very hard to block those memories out of my mind. Those memories involved early molestation from my uncle; touching me and placing his penis between my legs, not penetrating but creating enough friction that he would climax. After cleaning me off, he would send me out of his room to go outside and play with the other kids in the home. I could remember not wanting to be left alone in the home with my uncle because I feared what he would do, and I did not like it. I really did not understand what he was doing to me and why he was doing it. At our home, my mother kept me very sheltered. How ironic this was since every time I was sent to my grandmother's home, I was molested, fondled, and made to feel dirty. As I got older, he finally left me alone. I never told my mother what was happening to me. I only told her that I did not want to go back down to my grandmother's home. I would cry and beg her to let me stay in New York. My mother never got it.

The time I almost died, was the time I had to spend a whole school year at my grandmother's because we had a house fire in New York. We lost everything except for the clothes on our backs and a few things we could salvage from the fire. For about a week, my mother and I lived in the shelter similar to a hotel and it was really a dangerous place for a mother and daughter to live. We had to constantly watch over the few possessions we had left as to not lose them to thieves. My mother decided it was best for me to leave Brooklyn, New York until she could get another place to stay. I begged my mother to contact my father, but out of just sheer anger at my father, she said he did not want me. Thus, her decision was to send me to her mother for a year. I was distraught because I really hated being in Selma, Alabama in my grandmother's home. But what could I do, tell her the truth about why I did not want to go stay with my grandmother; not an option. So my 10th grade year was spent in Selma, Alabama. This is an important statement because for my entire life after I left that very example of hell, I blocked that entire year out my mind and denied that year ever existed. It was the worst year of my entire life. That year was filled with mental abuse from my grandmother and cramped living conditions because I slept in the bed with my two aunts, who at that time, still lived in the home. The sexual molestations began again. This time, at the hands of another uncle who came back home to live, as though there were not already enough people in that small, light green house, with a trailer home in the backyard occupied by my mother's older brother and his family. This uncle would sit in the dark living room at the front part of the house and wait for me to come down the hall to enter the kitchen or to fetch something my grandmother requested. He would grab me and hold me tight and rub on my body in places where an uncle should not touch his niece, then when he heard someone else coming, he would let me go. I stayed in fear of having to move around the house by myself, not knowing when I would get molested and rubbed upon. My mother would call, but my calls were supervised by my grandmother to ensure I did not say anything that would cause her to lose the money my mother was sending her. Each day I stayed in that home, the more my body began to shut down. I began to contemplate suicide, my menstrual cycle stopped, I lost so much weight and I just walked around numb and afraid to feel.

I began to reach out to my dad because even though my dad and mom never got married or lived together, he was always in my life. I always knew my dad loved me and I always felt like daddy's little girl. My dad saved my life!! The sad thing is that my dad died never knowing that he saved his daughter's life by recognizing something was wrong in her voice. My dad said one day- "is everything okay?" I said, "No". He said "do you want to leave and come stay with me?" I said, "Yes, but she will not let me". My dad said "I am sending you a plane ticket and when school is out, you will come stay with me". My dad told my grandmother that she better put me on the plane. School let out and I was heading to Dunn, North Carolina the very next day. My grandmother made my last few months worse than I could have imagined. My mother was mad that I had involved my dad. Finally, I was feeling a reason to live. So you see, if my dad had not listened to the pain and anguish in my voice and taken action, I would not be here today; nor would my son. My whole present and future would not exist. It took me about four months before my body relaxed enough, and before I truly felt safe enough that my body resumed its natural functions, including the return of my menstrual cycle.

DOMESTIC ABUSE

Domestic abuse is the mental and physical abuse that someone encounters at the hand of someone they love, a significant other or spouse. It is so amazing to me when I hear women say that will not happen to me. Why? Because I thought I was one of those strong women, but it did happen to me. In my early twenties, I became a victim of domestic abuse. Of course it did not start that way. He was funny, nice and persistent. We worked together at the Sharon Harris Nuclear Power Plant as armed security guards. We were together for almost five years; the first year plus some months was great!! We got engaged and then things began to change. He became very possessive and began trying to isolate me from family and friends. If we went out and someone looked at me, it caused an argument. I somehow was responsible for the unsolicited stares from other men. If anyone complimented me, it caused an argument. One day during a heated argument he hit me, and we literally fought like two strangers. The next day, he apologized and said that would not happen again, but he lied. He would buy me a gift, then turn around in rage and break it. He punched holes in the walls of our home, but I would not shrink into helplessness. I was a fighter and would always hit back but that only made the bruising worst. He would tell me, that the only way I could leave him was through death. That part scared me and that caused me to stay longer than I should have stayed in such a mentally and physically damaging environment. The turning tides came when it began to affect our work environment to the point of almost losing our jobs. There I sat, in one of our observation rooms with another officer monitoring the perimeter. My then fiancé came in the observation room at the very moment when the co-worker told me he liked my new look because I was wearing make-up. My fiancé stated that I looked like a whore and slapped me in front of our co-worker. I jumped out of my chair, grabbed a pair of scissors and headed over the railing to stab him in his back as he walked out the door. At that moment I did not care about job or consequences, I just wanted him dead. The co-worker jumped out of his chair and caught my arm as it was coming down and stopped the scissors from stabbing my fiancé. Of course a report was written on the incidence and what followed next was a one-week suspension for both of us. The day I left this man I made it up in my mind that I would rather die than to stay in such a relationship. He chased me through the streets of Erwin with a shotgun to scare me, but he realized I was ready to die; he drove home before I could make it home, and locked all doors. I had my dad and the cops to meet me at what was *my* home so I could safely remove my things. The days to follow were filled with him trying to intimidate me with his presence, but it eventually tapered away to nonexistence. Domestic violence is not something to be attributed to the weak; it is something that sneaks up on you like a predator; subtle and at times deadly. Mine was not unto death, but so many women have died at the hands of their domestic abuser.

RAPE

    Many think rape only comes at the hands of a stranger, but this is so far from the truth. My rape came at the hands of my ex-boyfriend while we were both in the military. We were separated for a while before he contacted me to talk about working on our relationship. My son at the time was very young and was always with me because I feared he would become a victim of molestation. My ex-boyfriend and I started talking in an open area and he seemed so kind and so trust-worthy. So when he invited my son and I back to his place to eat dinner with him and his two sons, of whom he now had custody, I agreed. After dinner, we continued to talk until late into the evening. My son, was in the room playing with his two boys and I was sure that he was tired. My ex-boyfriend offered for us to stay the night and stated that my son could sleep in the room with his two boys and I could have his room. He stated he would stay in the living room and I could even lock his door. Everything appeared safe, so I agreed. My son was asleep in the other room next door when I woke up to my ex-boyfriend pinning me down to the bed. My ex-boyfriend was about 6'3" and very strong and fit. I tried to fight back by moving and wiggling but I could not get him off me. I wanted to scream but he reminded me of my son in the next room sleeping. Before I knew it, he was inside me thrusting as I tried to push him off crying, and begging him to stop in a low voice, scared to wake and frighten my son. Once he was finish, he got up and walked out the room stating he will always be in my life because I will be carrying his baby. I lay in his bed until the next morning scared that he would hurt my son if I tried to leave before the morning. That night caused me to have to make difficult decisions I think about and constantly ask God's forgiveness for, but I only have one child and I am not bound to him. I never told anyone about the rape because I felt it was my fault going to this man's home. I put my child and myself in danger trusting that man. I questioned- was I so naïve and weak that I allowed this to happen to me? Victim; again to another man, when will I stop being a victim to men? So I stayed silent, yet again, holding in what was really happening to me and in me.

SURVIVOR

Throughout my life I have had to battle against men to survive. Whether it was the molestation by my uncles, the domestic violence by my fiancé, battling for respect in the military to be heard and respected, or the rape by my ex-boyfriend while I was in the military; I have had to fight for not just my life, but also my sanity. My paternal grandmother introduced me to God. Although my maternal grandmother went to church and was on all the committees, she did not have any of His qualities. I thank God for my paternal grandmother because she was an example of God's love and the reason why I know Him!! I knew if I could just get to know God, I could get through anything. Prayer has been my lifeline and my assurance that I am never alone. Knowing God has given me the understanding that in order to come out as pure gold, you must go through the fire. Looking back on everything I endured, I could see God's hand opening doors to get me out of the hell I was experiencing right here on earth.

Today my faith is stronger than ever, because I am a living witness of God's saving grace. So when you read my story, don't feel sorry for me because I am so much more than the pain I experienced. See, my strength which is God, He allowed me to *press* into the person I am today and the person I will be in the future. See the college graduate which holds a Master's Degree in Human Resources. See the mother of a son who is in college, and praise God, never had trouble with the law. See the retired Army Veteran. See the entrepreneur of her own company, Bootz to Heelz and a couple of other affiliated multilevel businesses. See the speaker. See the author who has currently co-authored two books. When you read my story, see yourself overcoming your past and stepping into your future-victorious and empowered! I tell my story to let you know you do not have to be a victim of your past; you can use your past to make you triumphant over your future.

To God Be The Glory!

PURPOSE REFLECTIONS:

- Your Past Does Not Define Your Future or You. You can rise above your past and soar into your future.
- God is always in the midst; even when circumstances look dark. Just keep praying and believing and the light will appear.
- You are never to blame yourself for the negative things that occurred to you, such as rape, molestation, or domestic abuse.
- Don't hold in your traumas. Speak about them, especially to the ones that love you!! Communication is very important.

Strength comes through pressing. Courage comes through movement. Healing comes by recognizing you are strong and courageous.

A REASON TO BE

Greatness comes from living with Purpose and Passion

A REASON TO BE VOLUME 3

Author Tammie T. Harris

Tammie T. Harris

Tammie T. Harris is a native of Rocky Mount, North Carolina by the way of Greenville, North Carolina; she resides in Wake Forest, North Carolina. Tammie and her husband Adam, are Pastors of New Seed Ministries in Raleigh, NC. Her goal is to see people experience wholeness in every area of their lives. Her theme for life is- Let the living begin, Be Healthy, Wealthy & Wise! She is an encourager and motivator! Her ministry gifts encourage people to Grow, Develop & Change to be made whole where there is nothing missing and nothing Broken. To live their best lives in the earth. Tammie and her husband have three wonderful sons Michael 29, Aaron 27 and Jalen 17 and a beautiful daughter-in-law Shinqua 28.

With many qualifying experiences, believing in family and community, Tammie has been assisting families with meeting life goals for over thirty years. Tammie has worked with a private non-profit organization as a Clinical Coordinator for In-Home Counseling programs, where she managed 14 programs throughout Eastern North Carolina. Tammie also served in many volunteer positions: Habitat for Humanity, The Executive board for The International Alliance of Christian Business Women, Economic Development Ministry, Family Counseling Center & Real-Estate Development Ministry for World Overcomers Christian Church. She served on Wake County PTA groups and as the Kids Vote Coordinator. Tammie has participated in BNI Business Networking International. She is a member of The International Alliance Christian Business Women. Tammie is a licensed Real Estate professional and owns The Tammie Harris Group LLC with ReMax One Realty in Raleigh North Carolina. She is a Member of the North Carolina Association of Realtors as well as the National Association of Realtors. Her Team of Real Estate specialist includes working with foreclosures, investors, estate sales and listing homes as well as working for buyers to purchase homes.

Tammie is a Licensed and Ordained Pastor, she holds a Certification in Pastoral Counseling from Virginia Union School of Theology, Bachelor of Arts in Sociology from Shaw University, Associate Degree in Computer Science from Phillips Jr. College, Interviewing Certification from University of North Carolina at Chapel

Hill University and was a graduate of the Community Fellow Leadership Graduate Program from the Down East Partnership for Children. She attended JY Monk Real-Estate School in order to obtain her license as a professional Real-Estate agent. She has served as Broker-In-Charge in the Real-Estate world. Tammie is a Graduate of Joseph Business School out of Chicago, Illinois.

Rags to True Riches

"Whoever can be trusted with very little can also be trusted with much, and whoever is dishonest with very little will also be dishonest with much. 11 So if you have not been trustworthy in handling worldly wealth, who will trust you with true riches? 12 And if you have not been trustworthy with someone else's property, who will give you property of your own?" (Luke 16:10-12 NIV)

I have started looking at life, like chapters in a book. I think I started saying that when I was approaching 50. I thought - "Wow, I've had several different lives. I've been, married, single, separated and divorced. I've birthed a child, miscarried a child, and buried another child. I've been poor and I've been wealthy. I've been elated with joy, but I've also been so disappointed by life that I felt my mind slipping away. But what all these things had in common was me and my years of these vast experiences that brought me to this place called *here!* I call it my Zoey life where there's nothing missing and nothing broken. Not a perfect place at all, yet a combination of enough experiences for me to know that there is a God who is on my side. A God that restores!

I recall when I was a little girl about eight years old, my grandmother Ella Jane firmly, and unapologetically told me that I would be someone special in life and that I would do something great. All the while I'm thinking in my mind- "No, not me. I'm being abused right now as she tells me this and I'm thinking, how in the world will I be able to be anything other than this *dirty, unattractive* little girl. I had no idea that my grandmother was prophesying into my life; that she heard a word from God that would change my destiny as she began to declare and decree over my future. That was the first few chapters of my life; learning that bad things do happen to good people, but it doesn't mean that it will always be that way.

As time passed I began to realize that the sum total of my life would happen over a lifespan and not just during my teen years. Growing up really poor and having moved a total of 27 times in my whole life is still mind blowing to me. We weren't a military family; it's just that at least eight of those times, it was because the rent was late, or my parents couldn't pay it, or we were pad- locked out by the sheriff's office. We were just poor. My family were former sharecroppers who were no longer farming and had to provide housing for themselves with jobs outside of the farm life. They had moved from a very rural area to a more urban location where you needed additional skills to get a job that paid well. I was blessed that I gave my life to Christ at the young age of 14, because it gave me a better perspective on being thankful *in-spite* of life circumstances. My faith kept me from the full impact of many additional disappointments. This new relationship with God gave me peace in the midst of storms and it helped me to understand that God had a plan for my life in spite of what I was experiencing. During this time, I would live off and on, with my auntie to baby-sit and so that I could graduate from the same high school I had been attending. This was necessary because we had moved once again. My auntie was a go- getter, hard worker, drove new cars and she was a homeowner. She was my first person, up close and personal, that I saw was successful. Living with her and watching her was such a great *shaping* experience for me. As a result, it became clear in my mind that there had to be more in life than struggling and being poor.

As time grew, I became motivated and planned on attending college after graduation. I remember a family member saying that I wasn't *college material;* so here comes a whole new chapter of my life which introduced me to more fear, doubt and unbelief in a whole different way. I wondered would I measure up. I wasn't a good student in high school, so I wasn't sure about college, but I knew I had to do something different to move beyond where I was. My mother may have been poor in resources but she was rich in words and love. Flat-footed, she said to me-, "You will do well in college and you are smart". She introduced me to the concept of looking at myself in the mirror and singing this song that she made up called - *I look good to myself!* I didn't believe my affirmation, but because I remembered what my grandmother had told me and the words of my mother, I just decided to *fake it until I could make it.* I didn't always see myself as smart, nor did I think that I was attractive and I certainly didn't make all of the right choices during those seasons. However, I gained strength through relationships that validated who I was as a person and who I was becoming. I called that my 20th something chapters. A few years after college, I'm married and was on my way! My whole life changed. I'm a wife, mother, had a wonderful career as a social worker, lived in a gated community and traveled well. I thought- "Finally, in spite of small beginnings, I'm living my dream life. I'm not poor anymore and I see myself winning after all of the struggling, abuse and low self-esteem." Little did I know that the dream would come crashing down!

In the 30th something chapters, I'm welcoming my second child into the world and she was going to be my *mini me*, but instead, at

22 weeks I'm delivering a still-born. That changed me forever. A year later, with great hopes of restoration, I'm pregnant again, but find myself having a miscarriage on Mother's Day and thinking- "God, you must have a interesting sense of humor because who could even make this stuff up." I truly felt blindsided because I never thought anything like that would happen to me. Needless to say, although I had life all planned out, it wasn't working the way that I thought it would. So much had taken place in those years; way too much to name, the good, the bad and the ugly. Losing children in a marriage is never easy and the grief alone has a toil that no one really understands. So after 18 years with the same guy, it ended just like that. I felt major failure, rejection and loneliness.

Headed toward my 40th something chapter, I'm a single mother, no longer living in a gated community, one income with negative balances in my checking account, dating again as an adult, low on strength and time. Yet, I was still remembering what my grandmother and mother told me all those years before. By this time, I had known what it felt like to be without money as a kid, then having money as an adult, to now feeling like I'm back at square one! What I did know was that having money just felt so much better. My son was five years old and at that age, he really didn't understand all that was taking place. This spared me and my son some of the pain that he would have experienced in the divorce process. I had never ever thought I would be a single mother raising a male child. I told myself that my son would not be a statistic and nor would I. All I knew at that moment was that life and circumstances had a way of switching up plans on you, but I still had hope in God that somehow I knew He would take what the enemy meant for evil and work it for my good.

So here I was *single,* sometimes sad and certainly wanting more for my life and for my son, I knew something had to change. I had been working in my field of study which was social work/family therapy, but since everything around me was changing I began to ask myself- "What would I do career wise if I wasn't afraid? Where would I live if I wasn't afraid? Maybe I needed a change. I got my answer as I prayed and listened. I went to real-estate school and got my broker's license, moved to a new city, had a townhome built in Knightdale North Carolina, near Raleigh, North Carolina where I always wanted to live since college; I started over from scratch. I didn't know a soul there at that time but I was determined my son's life would matter and that he nor I, would become just another number with a tragic end. It was all new, but I kept saying -*yes* to God even in a cloudy place, and even if it would cost me everything, I still told God- *yes*. And just like that, one day I realized I'm not afraid to live and I'm not afraid to die! I had been through all types of heartbreaks, betrayal, abuse and disappointment. Yet I was still standing, still trusting and still believing! So I decided I had nothing else left to fear because God was faithful. As quick as I remembered being in deep despair and disappointment; it seemed just as quickly that I was in full bliss with an overwhelming sense of peace, joy and happiness! I've had seasons where I've experienced the best of times and the worst of times, all at the *same* time. I can truly say that my life is barely recognizable in terms of where I've come from. In the midst of it all, my attitude has had a way of remaining optimistic in spite of the circumstances that I met in each chapter of my life. I kept saying- *yes* when I really wanted to say- "Nope, I'm tired and I'm done!" I kept saying *yes* to God when everything around me was bleak. Crying, but still saying- *yes!*

Disappointed and even mad at God in certain seasons but still saying-*yes*. Funny story, I remembered a former coworker introducing me at an event and describing me as the little girl digging through horse maneuver with a good attitude because she was certain that there must be a toy in the midst of all of the waste! At the time I didn't think it was a great way to introduce me but I began to realize many years later that he was right. That's who I was, that's who I've always been, because I keep looking for the good in spite of the bad in people, places and things that had happened in my life. It was a gift from God that sustained me during the horrible chapters. There have been many days during my struggles that I felt God had simply left me; yet something deep inside said He was with me and that I could trust his hand!

Somewhere along the way, I began to understand that different chapters in the book of my life would bring me different opportunities to learn, grow, develop and change. Sometimes with great experiences and sometimes with things so wicked that you wouldn't wish it on your worst enemy! But I survived, and now I thrive! I do have *a reason to be!* I have a word of hope, that in spite of your experiences, your story isn't over until you say it's over and even then, at that time, God will remind you that He's not done with you yet. So your story is just starting. I know what it feels like to be violated and to be bound, but I also know what it's like to be so free to love yourself that even if there's no one else there to love and accept you, you are simply just fine.

Now about that money thing! Yes, I've been *stupid poor;* where I've had to wash my clothes daily in order to have something to wear the next day. Yet now I can say that I'm so wealthy, mentally & materially, that I lay in bed with tears thinking- "God you did this just for me. There's nothing that I wish for, that I don't have. I simply have more than enough and I have the tangible manifestation of his promises. I remember the day that I got the letter from my real-estate franchise that I had reached over the million-dollar mark in my income of revenue, all I could do was cry, because I'm that little girl from the trailer park, to the projects and now living in Prominence! Unapologetically, I say, don't quit, don't give up and please by all means don't faint! For in due season you will reap a reward! Now years later, totally restored and renewed in my 50th chapter living life like it's golden, I am a licensed and ordained Pastor with my husband who loves and adores me, A business owner with a dynamic & prosperous real-estate career, a mother of three wonderful sons and a beautiful daughter- in- law. I'm that daughter who can afford to pamper her parents with all of the love and gifts that they can imagine, a friend too many, but most importantly, I can say that I like and love me with my whole heart, and that after all of the storms and tests, God himself kept me with his right hand, so I will not complain. So much good has happened in my life that many days I just stand in sheer amazement. Life is good. I remember one day saying- "What do you do after the dream?" This chapter here, feels so good, in spite of all it took to get me here. I'm grateful, thankful and glad that I made it! I'm up in these chapters living life like it's golden and I would not take "nothing for my journey". So, to those who are reading this, just know that if you don't quit, you will win. You still have time to thrive. Your best days are still ahead of you. God has way more in store than you can ask, imagine or think about. And yes, I'm looking in that mirror, Mama, I'm singing the song that you wrote- *I look good to myself!*

The End

Author Teresa Howard

Teresa Howard

Teresa Hawley Howard is an international author and publisher. She wants to use her life to inspire and encourage others. Her mission is to help ten thousand to find their voice and share their story. She is married to a wonderful man, Rickey. She is a mom and a *Mimi*. She knows your words have power!

Website: teresahawleyhoward.com
Email: teresa@takeactionwithteresa.com

My Pain Became My Purpose

Each of us is born with a purpose. A reason we are supposed to be in this world at this time. Some of us know our reason at birth. It is nurtured by those around us. They see a light in us and kindle it, fan it and help it grow. They know we are meant for greatness! They make sure we get the training, the schooling and connections we need to succeed. But it is not like that for all of us! It was not like that for me. My reason, my purpose came from pain. It came from betrayal and hurt. It came from an unspeakable and dark space. But it is my purpose and my reason to be in this world. I am going to share it with you in my chapter.

I was only eleven when my innocence was stolen. It was taken in on swift move by a man my mother trusted, loved and was married to. She never considered this man would hurt me. That he would damage me. That he would take my childhood and my future. That one action from him would change the entire course of my young life. Now you may be thinking, how do you recover from that? How do you move on? How do you heal from such a horrific event? Let me tell you; only with God. I was lucky; I had grandparents who stepped up. I know you are thinking after this event how can I call myself lucky. But I was. I have seen as a Court Appointed Special Advocate (CASA) volunteer, hundreds of children who had no one to step up. So, I was blessed with grandparents willing to take me, love me, guide me and help me heal.

At first, I was ashamed; I never spoke of it. I went back to school like everything was the same. But I was not. As I look back at the pictures, I can see the changes. The smile is gone. No longer do I take pride in dress or appearance. I don't want anyone to notice me. I am silent in class. I do maintain my all A-average. But I am no longer interactive with classes and projects. I wanted to melt into the wall paper.

Fast forward five years; I'm in high school. I don't date. I don't really talk to boys. I hang with an older crowd. I am looking for security. For a protector. For someone older to keep me safe. And I am sure I found him. He's twenty-five years old and I am barely sixteen. But he says he loves me and that is all it takes. I marry him. I have two beautiful girls with him. But he is not my protector; not my savior. He becomes my abuser. A new kind of betrayal and pain. He is emotionally abusive. He is physically abusive. He is mentally abusive. He makes my life, a time filled with agony, pain and shame. He is controlling and mean; I fear him. I stay twenty plus years trying to make it work and have him love me. The problem is, I don't know what love is. I have never seen it, felt it or known it. I am ashamed, broken and tired. Most of all tired. I am tired of just existing, tired of just being, tired of having no purpose.

Then a woman speaks a word into me. A spark to a nearly dead life and existence. She tells me I deserve more. I don't believe her but I am honored that she thinks that. She sits by me in church. She has no idea what is happening in my home. She has no idea what is happening to me personally. And she has no idea of what I have been through. But she tells me, God told her to tell me I am his child! That I have a father. It's a key that opens a flood gate. She has no idea my father was a drug dealer and heroine addict. She has no idea that he is dead. And that my husband loved to torture and hurt me by telling me I was fatherless. That not even my father loved me or cared enough to stick around and protect me. She has no idea her words are like rain on the desert. That they are pouring over me and filling all those cracks and empty places. She is only being obedient to God. It is my miracle.

I get up enough courage to leave. And I leave everything behind. My girls are grown. So, I start from scratch. From nothing! At the time, I thought- "God, why? Why am I having to begin again with nothing. No money, No job, No place to live, No thoughts on what to do". But now I know it is because God had greater plans for me. And God did not want any person to be able to take credit for what he was about to do in my life.

Fast forward nine years. I am whole, I am healed, I am a child of God and I am strong enough to live again. My home is paid for. My cars are, too. I make my living doing what I love and helping others to heal from their pain, too. I am completely blessed! God turned it all around! He showed me how to take what the devil meant to destroy me and use it for his glory. I use my pain and past to help others heal and overcome! I help others speak their truth and know their worth. I know my reason to be! Do you? I pray you do. I pray you are walking in your purpose and using your gifts.

PURPOSE REFLECTIONS

There are 5 things I want you to take away from my story:

1. You are worthy. Do not let anyone tell you differently.
2. You are meant for a purpose in this world.
3. You are here to inspire, encourage and change the world.
4. Your pain is not forever. You can heal and walk through it.
5. Your words and obedience to God can change someone's life completely!

So, choose to speak up. Choose to be the change. Choose to be a voice for the voiceless. Choose to embrace your *reason to be*! Choose to follow your passion! Know your purpose and walk in it daily.

Author Peggy B. Jones

Peggy B. Jones

To Thine Own Self Be True, is a quote that has carried her all of her life. Reverend Peggy B. Jones has become true to who she is. She is a genius within her own tribe; emerging out of poverty to find and clarify her purpose to find her REASON TO BE. Peggy has redefined her value, as well as her abundant life.

Dr. Peggy Jones is an ordained pastor and the founder of Marriage School, a ministry that informs, instructs, and inspires to promote healthy relationships. Peggy is a motivational speaker, self-taught interior decorator and President and Founder of Christian Women in Unity Women's Ministry; a ministry that has been established for over 33 years. She is a Woman-to-Woman Pastor, mentor and P4 Certified Life Coach.

Dr. Jones is also wife to Charles H. Jones, for over 46 years and mother of three genius sons and six grand geniuses.

What's Going on In This House?

My address was 902 Faison Street. Something within me knew this house would be the house I would be in until I would leave. I was in the fourth grade. My teacher lived right next door. Initially, I wasn't sure if that was good or bad; but throughout the years it was good. I was happy to be in the new house because we had always lived in an apartment with neighbors living in adjoining apartments, right next door; but it seemed like it was the next *room*, and that was too close for comfort," as my mom used to say.

Today, I look at so many houses and apartments and I wonder; what goes on in there? What's happening throughout the night when all neighbors are sleep and minding their business. Just like you can't tell a book by looking at its cover; you can't tell a family by looking at the outside of their house. We were surrounded by upward mobile families. Doctors, teachers, contractors, and state workers. Unlike them, my family was blue collar workers; working more than one job at a time. We lived among families who had four, five, and some with ten or more children; it seemed they were always well fed and provided for. We were just a family of four, with my brother and me being the only kids. Yet, we were always lacking; always in need of something that was normal for most families to have. My brother and I didn't have an answer to why we did not have or could not have like the other families. *Lack* became our normal. I had become an expert in accepting *no* as the answer to most requests. I'm amazed how memories of my past stay so close to me. It seemed as though we lived in a prison of reality. It looked happy and normal but it was so painful. There was nothing you could do about it except "adjust yourself, don't complain and count your blessings."

I learned to do that so well. Eventually, there was not a desire in me to ever have anything. "What's the use?" I always thought. I remember that at Christmas time, my dad would bring home the Sears and Roebuck catalogs. You would have thought he had brought home, *gifts* out of the catalog. But it was exciting, and that's all we had. I learned to visualize a home with my own room; decorated in "100 percent Girl." I shopped for toys I could choose without cost. I chose the clothes I could never have except in my imagination. I created a secret space where everything could be kept until I could grow up and provide them for myself. Maybe not today but I bet on my life that I would have those things and more someday. My bro and I will look together and say- "I'm getting this or that," but we both knew that not one thing we turned pages to see would be for us. Not one thing! Another game we learned to play!

Promises, promises!

Hope deferred makes the heart sick, but when the desired comes, it is a tree of life. I kept waiting for the one day things would be better". A promise from the promise-keeper of whom I had yet to know. The only promise-keeper I knew was my Mother Ma. If she promised us something, she would die if she did not do it. I learned how to keep promises by observing my mother. Her word of promise was the definition of integrity however; unlike the promise-keeper,

Mom had only a small bag of promises, which she kept close to her heart because she knew her children lived in the same world of disappointment as she did. Promises helped keep us from dying of sadness, disappointment and hopelessness. My Mom had a small bag of promises, she loved us unconditionally, and she tried to protect us as much as she could.

There was joy in our home with my Mom no matter what we had or did not have. Her covering love and protection for us canceled out every bad thing. When disappointments came, my Mom would tell us- "Don't stay there, you got to learn how to move on when things don't turn out the way you hoped they would." In other words, get over it quickly! My Dad would come home, and it would be a brand-new storm that blew in; time to come to attention and listen for new orders. My father was a military man, and he treated us like enlisted men. Whatever he said went, didn't matter if he's home or gone, he demanded the same respect! Something new was up.

Guess who's coming to visit?

One day my Dad came home after being missing for a few days and nights and announced that his oldest brother, Uncle James would be coming to stay with us. Uncle James was 6.5 over 300 pounds and was being released from Cherry Hospital, the mental hospital which we called the "crazy house." Oh no! How's that going to work! Why our house, we have no room! My brother and I had twin beds. I had to give up my bed for Uncle James. Our lives were about to change and I didn't know how much until the day he arrived at 902 Faison Street.

My mother had the burden of taking care of us and now another burden of caring for the *unknowns* of her brother-in-law. My Dad said "he's my brother and my family, we take care of family." And we are family too, but he was not taking care of us. Dad would leave us with his brother; he would leave us alone to care for him. During this time, we had little food in the house and we were hungry. My mother, my brother and I were the new caregivers to a mentally ill patient. We had no idea what that really meant for us, but we would soon find out.

19 days

It had been only 19 days since I graduated. Somehow, I had fulfilled the wishes of my father; to go to school and make good grades and get my high school diploma. I did that, but what would be next? There was a scholarship for me for a summer program at the North Carolina School of the Arts, at Winston Salem. My homeroom teacher had gotten the scholarship for me. I was a creative dancer for my high school. This summer program was the one thing I could participate in that cost me nothing. I had a chance to possibly go to college. My head was spinning at the thought of such a wonderful possibility. I could finally leave home and make a life for myself.

Going to college?

I was given a folder with an application for my Mom to sign and attach, a money order of five dollars?! My head began spinning and suddenly I became so afraid. The reality of what poverty and lack was, stood in front of my face. Yes, my mother would be so proud of me and so happy for me, but she would be so disappointed because she did not have five dollars for the application fee. I knew this all too well. My mom had always kept my brother and me informed on the next crisis in our family. It was a weekly briefing. This week, no lunch money, next week no sandwiches, next week we won't have this, that, or the other. We were always prepared to have some kind of lack in our lives. This was our normal. As I slowly walked home that day, what had started out as great news, and great expectations, soon became a dead dream, awaiting a graveside funeral service.

As I walked up the steps of 902 Faison Street, I knew there was no five dollars, no clothing for me to put in a suitcase I didn't have, no ten dollars to get me on a bus to the campus and no financial support when I got there. This idea made no sense to me. I wanted to believe that something good was happening for me, who had nothing but lack, but my heart was failing from what I knew to be true. Before I opened that door, I had to make a decision and I did!

My mother would, if she could, make a way for me to go. I knew she couldn't and I couldn't put her through the stress of trying to find money for me to go to school even with the scholarship. My dad would tell us when we couldn't pay the light bill and the lights would be turned off for a few days. He would say, we are just going through a hardship right now. I did not want to cause a hardship for my family and especially not for my mom who was always in a "hardship." Neither my mom nor my dad ever knew about the scholarship. The moment had come and gone in a matter of minutes; not even my best friend knew about the scholarship. I've kept this all of my life. It didn't matter if you couldn't afford it. I told my teacher that I couldn't go because it would be too much of a hardship for my family, and I thanked her and explained that talking to my parents would not help.

Make a decision

I had to make another decision in my head, because things were about to change again. I can't go to college. I am not going to the military; I was going buddy/buddy with my best friend, but she got pregnant, so that was not happening. What was going to happen was that I would be leaving this place of poverty, lack and hardships. This was their life, but it's was not going to be mine. I was going to New York City to live there, to work there, and to make it there! The bus fare was $18.50 from North Carolina to New York City. I had absolutely no money and knew that I had to raise it myself. I had to figure this out and I had 19 days to do it. In 19 days it would be Father's Day and 19 days earlier was my graduation day. Twelve years of school; graduation had finally come, but my dad made a decision not to show up. Since my dad made a decision not to show up, Father's Day seemed like a good day to start a new life. And I did.

My jobs to fund my new life:

No one was going to give me any money, I had to earn it. And we were taught never to ask for money. I had babysat for my next-door neighbors. I had been an assistant driver for my fourth grade teacher. I would ride with her to the A&P and help her with bags and help her park. I remember Ms. Harris driving 15 mph and when she would go 25mph she would say with a big grin, "Oh, we are sailing now". Mrs. Catherine lived across the street from 902, she had beautiful black silky hair and although she had eleven children, she would ask me to scratch her head. An art some know of and most will never know. Many times I would scratch her head to get money to go to the swimming pool. I also, would run to the store for her. I had to check with my former employers and I would ask if they had one more job for me because I had to raise my bus fare for my new life. I had to work for my bus fare. I did get the jobs and I made about $10. Still short 8:50, that's all I needed and I would be on the bus; or so I thought. Since my first bus ride away from home, I've seen many people travel with paper bags for suitcases, and greasy bags of food to eat while they traveled. I bet you didn't know what was going on in their houses that they would come as they were. I think I had an idea. They were leaving something; going to somewhere; hoping for something different. Not knowing what; but taking a chance.

I realized I didn't have a suitcase. I didn't have food to carry for the trip. I was just trying to leave something to go somewhere, to find a reason to be somebody. And perhaps they were as well. Sometimes, it becomes expedient that we leave certain people, places, and things in life. It's a call to attention, as your life begins to shift. You must be in step and keep up with everything that's within you. Get your orders and follow them, you cannot be afraid!

Cousin Ruby let me use her suitcase; everything I owned fit perfectly in it. I was very appreciative. The suitcase was light enough for me to handle without help. Cousin Ruby told me tales of life in New York City. She had lived there for years and had recently returned to North Carolina. There were rumors of her being run out of New York, and she was somewhat of a gangster. She would give me the rules of engagement with New Yorkers, "Don't Speak to everybody like we do in the South. Watch your pockets. They will rob you and you won't even know you were robbed. There are people from all over the world who live in New York and everybody that's friendly is not your friend. Trust nobody. Mind your business, and watch out for yourself. Get a good job, because there are plenty of jobs in New York". A job was my goal. I had to have a job so I could take care of myself and make enough money to go back home and get my mother away from her life of poverty and lack. A Job was what I was going for. I wasn't looking for love or a relationship. I wasn't looking for the same life I was leaving; I was looking for a different and more abundant life. I'll take over this life from here, I'll take care of my needs, I will eat what I need, I will provide for myself.

Part 3: My Disconnect

Once I knew I was not going to college, I felt a strong sense of disconnect from the place where I was born, bred and lived my entire life. Something was leading me not to remain in Wilson. I had no fear. What I didn't know I would figure out. I could read, write and I could think. When I would be disciplined, my Mom would say, "go sit down and think." I would and I would figure out what and why I was sitting and thinking. Think so you can make a decision and move on with your life. As I thought of my new life in New York, I stopped thinking that staying in Wilson could be an option. It was not an option. I had to leave. I didn't know what to expect, but adventure would be my middle name. I didn't have much in my life, but I always had something to read. And I read everything I could put my hands on: Readers' Digest, encyclopedias, weekly readers, school literature books, comic books, love and relationship books, geography books about other lands and people. Many of my father's friends were school teachers, and they would stop by at the end of the school year and bring me all these books that I could read and keep. Thank you, Mr. Charles Platter. The books became my friends and my tutors. These were thrown away books, but to me they were treasures. A book has always been an escape for me. The late Dr. Miles Monroe once said, "You only know what you have learned, but what you have learned is not all there is to know". This is a great lesson for me!

Keep learning and you will keep knowledge at the center of your life. As I go there will be so much more to learn.

My reason to be journey begins here. I have learned to be content in whatever state I find myself in; however, my shift into my purpose was finding my voice in my own story. Life has a way of trying the very substance of your being, and the journey that you take in life necessitates all that you have, have encountered, have endured, and have failed and succeeded. It takes all of you! I stand today rejoicing at the uncovering of the secret things of my life that have allowed me to discover ***my reason to be***. Hardships, tests, and trials did not break me nor kill me; it made me the woman I am today. What you have inside of you is greater than what lies outside of you. By the grace of God, the circumstances, the poverty, the disappointments, the shame and fears did not paralyze my life, neither will it yours.

It was God all the time. He allowed me to reach hundreds of people to share a message that will bring minds from poverty to an abundant life. It was good that I was afflicted that I might know God and his ways. If we can learn to make good decisions about our lives, we can move when opportunity presents itself or when opportunity changes.

God has allowed me to reach many people to help them to come out of a poverty mindset into the possibility of an abundant life. I would like to leave you with five mind shifts that many have used to become unstuck.

1. Have faith in God and God's word!
2. Be true to yourself!
3. Make a decision
4. Commit to personal development
5. Consider wcxfhat would you do or be if you were not afraid?

Who we are is not so easy to discover and know, but when we find the answer, our *reason to be* will be found as well!

Author Richard Joyner

Richard Joyner

Rev. Richard Joyner grew up in Greenville, NC, surrounded by farms, poverty, and anger. The son of a sharecropper, Joyner saw little apart from the white landowner whom he felt took advantage of his family. His father had a different perspective. "My father saw sustainability before I did," said Joyner "When anger blinds you, you can't see the whole thing."

In time, Joyner grew and evolved from angry son to minister and agricultural educator. He came to understand the importance of the land, of healthy lifestyles, and of relationships. As a result, Joyner helped one community become healthier, while giving hope to countless children.

After serving in the US Army and National Guard, Joyner attended divinity school at Shaw University and went to work as a chaplain at Nash General Hospital. In 2002, Joyner became the pastor of Conetoe Chapel Missionary Baptist Church, a church that serves an isolated community of approximately 300 residents.

In 2004, disturbed by the number of young people in his congregation who died of poor health, he founded the Conetoe Family Life Center, which works with young people in the community to plant, harvest, and sell healthy produce, a commodity previously scarce in rural Conetoe.

In recent years, the center has branched out to honey production. Participating students manage dozens of honeybee hives, paralleling Joyner's belief that people are "interdependent beings" who cannot reach their full potential without all members of a community reaching their potential, as well. "Every bee has a role," Joyner says. "And, in caring for the hives, the children see that they, too, have a role." It is a lesson that revolves around imparting a sense of community and helping young people understand how they can find both joy and sustainability in the land, just as Joyner once did.

Joyner was awarded the CNN HERO and is also an EMMY recipient.

The Land of Reason

No matter how hard we try to outrun our painful past, sometimes it stays with us for a reason. When I was a child, my father was a sharecropper. He worked hard sowing and tilling the land. At harvest time with his family by his side, he was so proud of what he had accomplished and then the owner would drive up, take everything away and tell him that they had earned nothing. That humiliation caused me so much pain that I hated that land and I left. I joined the military and later became a pastor and my calling led me to Conetoe, North Carolina, population 300.

I went there to preach. In one year I had presided over 20 funerals and that many of these deaths were preventable and could be stopped with healthier food. So I looked at the land and knew what I had to do. I started the Conetoe Family Life Center to grow fresh food. More than 80 young people in the area helped plan, plant and harvest nearly 50,000 pounds of produce a year for the local families and to raise money for school supplies and scholarships. My past stayed with me for a reason; to give me the strength to put the land to good use for its children and their future and for me to reconcile and heal.

The garden is really my sanctuary. It's where I come to watch God at work. I observe the little plant that just looked like it's not getting off. You nurture it a little bit and all of a sudden it catches, sprouts and grows. That's how life is. We were having untimely deaths, chronic diseases. I had to do something. Growing up, I didn't like farming. We were sharecroppers. It was painful. It still is painful. I just literally was praying one day and I really heard a voice that said, "Look around you". And really, there was nothing but land. I almost said, "Is there anybody else up there I can talk to"? But it was almost like my eyes opened up to the farm. Alright, come on guys. Who wants to do eggplants? It gave us the opportunity to create something that united us. It is intergenerational, but the children, they are the leaders in this process.

Once you cross I-95, coming east in North Carolina, the devastation will compare with a third world country. This was a textile area. Almost everybody here worked in the factories or the farm, period. Education was really not stressed that much. When the textiles left and the tobacco left, it left a huge gaping hole. Alcoholism, drug addiction, abuse, high school dropouts, teenage pregnancy, all this stuff. This is normal here in Conetoe. Because of the level of our pain unanswered, I believe that we have a level of addiction to match it. I really love being with the wounded. We make too many things a statistic; obesity, diabetes, high blood pressure. The people who have these chronic diseases, they shouldn't be victimized. Put people first and watch what happens. How do you feel about everything? Any concerns?

I personally started the Conetoe Family Life Center primarily as a response to a real crisis of diabetes, high blood pressure and untimely deaths in this area. Our mission here at Conetoe Family Life Center is to improve the health of our youth and the community. We do that by growing healthy foods, by educating the community about healthy living, empowering them to exercise every day. We don't judge, blame, or shame. We are just uniting to try to get to a place of sustainability for all of us. This is a food desert. The local people here do not have access to affordable locally grown foods.

The closest place to purchase food is about seven miles from here. Those needs really prompted us to begin to look at what is one way that we can address all of those issues and more. One of them is to produce our own food and at the same time unite us and to produce enough food to meet the needs of the community. Our centerpiece is our garden, but we also have to educate people about the nutritional value of the produce and how to prepare a balanced meal. So we have a very strong agri-business, coupled with our agriculture educational program that we teach throughout the year.

One of the programs that we are really proud of is our afterschool program. Sometimes that means taking a math problem and explaining a practical way of working it out or taking their biology assignment and cutting into a vegetable to examine the essential plant parts. It is classroom and application and they get to put it on their plate. The kids moved from our afterschool program into the summer camp, which is a little bit broader and a little bit more intense. We bring in specialists who are gifted in math and science and technology who will engage the kids throughout the summer in these programs. The camp is free. They don't have to pay anything and then they get breakfast, they get lunch, they have classes for them and sometimes we take them on trips. We started learning about bees and before I knew it, we had children that were certified as bee-keepers.

The kids also have an opportunity to work in the garden and they have an opportunity to earn money; money that go into a scholarship fund that they can draw upon when they graduate from high school. We do farm stands at Farmer's markets. If you leave it up to the youth, they are very creative. The will put a stand anywhere. This money is going back into the program and it's going back into scholarships and it's going back into our community. We are not building a corporation. We are building a community. Alright. I have worked tirelessly to ensure that these children don't get lost on the streets. I won't allow gangs or drugs to consume them. I get a chance now to mentor youth that I see have inherited pain that is generational

We say to our youth, "We will work with you so that your children will have a different opportunity than you have. We are going to walk with you through whatever is trying to rob you of your education. Together, we are going stop it". What started as a small youth development program in a very small community in eastern North Carolina turned into a program that feeds the poor and changes the lifestyles of the individuals that it has touched. I experienced the drudgery and disappointment of sharecropping, the death of my siblings, and rampant racism, I've watched that anger starting to deteriorate my own life. I really wanted to be a preacher; really wanted to be somebody to inspire people and was really excited about it, but it wasn't what I thought it was to be. It really wasn't helping people as much as I thought it would. The people that I met with to manage the church didn't seem like they had a compassion for the people. The focus was more on count the money, keep the building going, take out the money on Sunday. I kept trying to change that mindset and the more I tried the worse it got. So I left the church for a long time. I went to Nash Healthcare in 1999 as a community chaplain. I've been able to move from a community chaplain to a director of pastoral care, dealing a lot with hospice patients. The pastor that was here at the church in Conetoe, mentored me in my first ministry, so I came here to help him. He graciously accepted my support and went, "Well, good". Then, one Sunday, he came to church dressed up in a white suit and shoes and he introduced me as the pastor! I went like, "Whoa man, you can't do that". Then he said, "I'm 94 years old. I can do what I want to do". I fell in that role again of being that religious leader, but I was looking for another model. People needs really weren't being met. I needed a model that served the people.

Their light bills were due. You had comments, "Well, did he pay tithes or did he give to the church?" I'm like, "Well, that doesn't cut the lights back on". I was experiencing all of the deaths. I was experiencing all of the crisis and the needs. We needed something that would unite us and that would be sustainable. I thought, really sitting on the side of the road, 90-degree weather, hot, and I was just praying. I heard a voice that said, "Open your eyes and look around". There was nothing but fields and I was really like, "This is no time to play. Is there anybody else I can talk to? I don't like fields." I know that God isn't leading me back to a place that I am totally angry with. He was; he was leading me back to *me*. So that was the turning point. I personally started this center. We started out with a little plot of land and just a concept that we wanted to stop funerals and chronic disease in young people. We wanted to see our students stay in school, get a good education and we wanted to build a workforce. I invited children to come to help and a hundred children showed up.

They thought it was fun. I could've never bought this land. I could've never bought these tractors. I couldn't have bought any of this, but the relationships bought it all. So if we are going keep it, we've got to have relationships. We want to make sure that we provide all of the fresh, affordable, local grown vegetables that we can get on the table, of those in our community, because we believe that we can get our health back, Amen? Amen. We praise the Lord for that, that we can get our health back!

The hospital and the garden and the community for me, have become one. I get to go home with patients that are discharged. I get to go and sit in their homes. I get a chance to talk to the family. I get a chance to listen to the family. I can take food boxes with me. I can take recipes with me. I can even eat some of the food once they cook it, which they love to do for me. They love to say, "Hey, we prepared some food, are you going to stay for dinner?" I say, "Well, I didn't plan on leaving any way". Wedding on Saturday, funeral on Sunday and back at work on Monday, starting up the summer camp.

Every day with me starts at 3:30 in the morning. I've been really gifted with this rich privilege to find silence in places where it is sometimes so unusual to find it. Silence for me does not mean the absence of busyness. It means the presence of consciousness. I keep my bicycle in the car with me. So it's nothing to pull on the side of the road or find a place and park and just go for a great ride. Ride, yeah. It's like freedom to get out and ride and just enjoy it. I can hear things and I can breathe and I can get quiet time. I could be really tired, I'll look back in the back seat and see my bike and I go, "I've got to get a ride". And so I fell in love with bikes. It's one the expensive things that I have to repent on. I imagine Jesus saying, "I don't like you riding that bike. You need to give it up".

I'm 65 now. My father died at 64 and a lot of people in my family that are my age are battling some chronic diseases. So I changed my diet, I changed my mobility and it has given me a different outcome. We try to incorporate that into this community. My key role now, to be honest with you, is really to listen and my key role is to build relationships. I don't try to raise money. I don't try to put names on the roll. You don't have to sing in the choir. Let's really try to figure this out. How do we really help each other? That's what we've been doing for the last seven years, and it has been working for us, so it works for me. This community, this garden has changed me. I can preach from a place of love, unity and human development without condemning, blaming or shaming anybody. Now when I think I'm serving the less fortunate, the truth is, I'm the less fortunate. This community has given me a heck of a lot more than I have given it; a whole lot more. I have had the opportunity to be awarded the CNN HERO in 2015 and an EMMY by way of my *reason to be*.

Prayer has been my compass. I communicate to God daily, multiple times a day. Obeying the voice of God after I hear his voice. Trust God totally, He will never disappoint you. Life is precious. We took a huge barrier and transformed it into an opportunity. Our young people are leading us to a better place. They are growing beyond chronic diseases. They are going beyond disabilities. They are going way beyond those attitudes, we can't, we won't, and we don't have. They are strong and in charge. They are building the relationships, to each other, to the Conetoe family, to the land, and to their lives. It is a blessing to witness that to whom much is given, much is required. Fulfilling my requirement through service to my community is my *reason to be*.

Author Rhonda Kaalund

Rhonda Kaalund

Rhonda Kaalund is a graduate of Appalachian State University and a member of Delta Sigma Theta Sorority, Incorporated. With over 20 years of experience, Rhonda helps people defeat their emotional limitations through expressive arts, counseling, and life coaching. Through personal and professional development facilitation, Rhonda helps people build their confidence to meet their goals. Rhonda is the author of *From Invisible to Visible: Master the Art of Being Seen* and co-author of *The Love Pact*. Rhonda is also a Certified Laughter Yoga teacher where she uses aspects of laughter to help others cultivate happier meanings in life.

Facebook: https://www.facebook.com/rhonda.kaalund
Instagram: https://www.instagram.com/rhondakaalund
LinkedIn: https://www.linkedin.com/in/rhonda-kaalund-b20608141
Twitter: https://twitter.com/KaalundRhonda
Website: www.rhondapkaalund.com
Email: Rhonda@rhondakaalund.com

Happiness is a Choice

"That which does not kill me makes me stronger." -Friedrich Nietzsche

Growing up in the 70's was a happy time. It seems we had more fun back then. We played until the street lights came on, and when they did, we'd hang out a little longer on the front porch. Cell phones were unheard of, but talking on the kitchen phone with the long-coiled cord was cool. I remember, in order to make friends, we interacted in-person. And bullying back then was relegated to the girl who gave you a hard time because the popular boy liked you instead of her. Nonetheless, life was great, and I was happy.

My childhood was one which I'd return to again if I could. Momma would make these homemade peanut butter cookies and used a fork to crisscross designs on them. My sister and I would fight over who got to lick the spoon. Momma would make the best candy apples in the neighborhood. Not just the red ones, but blue ones, green ones and caramel ones. I can't forget the times shopping with Momma. She'd let us pick out our favorite cereal, and I'd run for the box of *Booberry*. And when no one was looking, I'd sneak a box of *Swiss Cake Rolls* in the cart and pretend my sister did it, even though she didn't like them.

Momma was my best friend. She was so beautiful. She was tall with flawless brown skin. She reminded me of Thelma from *Good Times*. Momma was from New York. She did everything fast. She talked fast and walked fast. I remember stumbling just to try to keep up with her. Momma made many sacrifices. She worked two jobs most times. We weren't rich, but we had what we needed and got what we wanted. On her days off, she'd play games with us. I was the master at jack rocks and hopscotch, my sister was the champion of double-dutch jump rope and no one could touch Momma's skills at Chinese checkers. Momma instilled great values in us. She'd always say, "Treat others the way you want to be treated," and "Don't pick at people." Considering the feelings of others was important in our house. If she caught my sister and I arguing or talking *ugly* to one another, she'd tell us to stop it or she'd go get a *switch*. In the back of our house, there were bushes where Momma could get a switch. So, we knew to get it together or Momma was gonna get us!

At around age five or six, Momma was trying to console me. I don't recall what was so upsetting, but I will never forget what she said. "Rhonda, happiness is a choice." Hmmm... "Happiness is a choice," I pondered. What did she really mean? I knew I liked the sound of it, but I didn't understand the caliber of influence those words would have over me. The one thing I did know, was that I preferred the happy, positive emotions. So, I made every effort to build a life around happiness.

Although we encountered trials; I learned to look at things from a different perspective. I learned to choose how I wanted to feel. I learned to sift out the lessons from the negative experiences and used them for opportunities for growth. I'd gotten so good at choosing positivity that bouncing back from adversity became second nature. Looking at things from a different perspective and choosing to feel positive emotions became the catalyst to my ability to be resilient.

Sticks and stones may break my bones

In 2018, my husband and I became co-authors in the book, *The Love Pact*. This book highlights eight couples who share their stories on marriage resilience. Our story focuses on marital bliss, despite having infertility challenges. I also published my first solo book, *From Invisible to Visible: Master the Art of Being Seen*. This book helps people who feel invisible, build the confidence they need to express the best version of themselves. I walk readers through an 11-step process called the REDLIPSTICK Method to achieve this. My emotional state was high, and I was feeling very blessed because I could use my books to help others heal. *From Invisible to Visible: Master the Art of Being Seen,* released as an international #1 Best Seller in four countries. My friend and I released our book around the same time, so we found ourselves spending countless hours each day checking for new reviews. Despite a handful of excellent reviews, I couldn't stop obsessing about the day someone would write YOUR BOOK SUCKS! Eventually, I got exactly what I had been obsessing over. It was there in black and white. A writer's nightmare! Two stars and countless insults jammed packed in a cozy paragraph available for any and every one to see. At first, I couldn't bring myself to read it, but I also couldn't bring myself to ask anyone else to read it. I cringed as I saw the words and phrases pop up: "exploits readers trust," "self-serving," and "phony." To see that, created the biggest lump in my throat. I literally could not swallow. My mouth went dry and I had a weird, unpleasant, tingling sensation that zipped through my body. It felt like someone had punched me in the chest. I could hardly breathe. The positive emotions that I had experienced moments earlier, disintegrated within an instant. My feelings of exhilaration quickly turned into humiliation. As a new author, what I wanted most was to have my book serve as a vehicle for healing and personal growth. Instead, my book had turned into rubbish. My reputation seemed shattered.

After seeing the feedback, I wondered who else saw it. I wondered if people believed what the person had written about me. I examined each sentence to see if there was any truth in it. The sentence or two about the actual book were fair; however, the three long paragraphs devouring my character held no merit. I was none of the things the reader called me. To try to get a better understanding, I reached out to the reader; only to be engaged in several days of email exchange which concluded with additional despicable insults. To survive the humiliation, I put on a facade. When people approached me about the attack, I tried to play it off as though it didn't matter; but to tell the truth, I could barely breathe. I was pretending everything was okay, but what I really wanted to do was go under a rock and hide. When I finally mustered up enough courage to talk about it with a few friends, they simply reminded me that I was now in the public eye and these kinds of things were to be expected. They all meant well, but at the time, I didn't need, nor did I want to hear that. In fact, I didn't know what I needed, but one thing was for sure; I was too embarrassed to speak with anyone else about it.

I knew things could get worse if I didn't get help; but the embarrassment of what was said, and the fear of judgement from reacting to such a "small" thing, simply had me wanting to go invisible. Someone attacked my character and left it for the world to see. This was new territory. I felt helpless and hopeless. I felt numb. I just wanted time to pass as quickly as possible and there was nothing anyone could say or do that could offer much comfort. I had trouble sleeping. I tossed and turned, and I couldn't get being called a "phony" out of my mind. I couldn't eat anything at first; then I found myself gaining weight from constantly overeating. My life had been totally disrupted. I even stopped going to the beach and taking pictures of the sunsets; one of my favorite things to do. My emotions were all over the place. I just couldn't get focused. Even when I walked through the grocery store, it felt like people were looking and saw "YOUR BOOK SUCKS" stamped across my forehead! So, to give comfort to this shame, I became muted.

I was too embarrassed to call it a traumatic experience because this wasn't a physical assault where I was left to die; it was simply someone who didn't know me, spewing an opinion about me. Despite the impact, it "seemed" small, however, I know now that my experience was traumatic. The old saying "Sticks and stones may break my bones, but words will never hurt me," was not true. What people say about us can affect us. I felt my career as a writer was over.

I spent some time wondering why this was so difficult. Why wasn't I able to bounce back from something that now seems so "small?" After all, happiness was supposed to be the choice for me. I prayed about why I was having such a hard time moving past this attack. It came to me that the fear of being judged was the real test. It was never about the intention of the person who wrote the message, but rather how I would handle the situation. Every situation we face in life, whether positive or negative, can be used for growth. We get to determine that. The opinion of others does not dictate our value or our worth. What I realized is that what we focus on, we bring into existence. My obsession and fear of being judged was so strong that I brought it into my existence. I called in that attack.

We must start thinking about, what we are thinking about. Are we focused on negativity? Are we focused on the absence of something? No matter what we are thinking about, our thoughts are powerful, and we have the power to bring into existence, that which we focus on, whether positive or negative. Therefore, we must be intentional about our thoughts. If we take the time to analyze what we think about the most, we should be able to see the connections with what has manifested in our lives. The times I chose happiness, I brought about positive experiences. This time, I didn't remember that I had the power to choose. I allowed the words of another person to dictate my emotional state. Words have the power to hurt, but they also have the power to heal; so, we get to choose how to interpret them. What others think about me is none of my business, and I want you to know that what others think about you should be none of your business, too. Therefore, we can conclude that sticks and stones may break our bones, but words should never hurt us.

Healing FACES

How did I heal from this situation? I prayed and meditated morning and night. I walked 30 minutes each day and listened to Dr. Wayne Dyers' book, *Change Your Thoughts Change Your Life*. I practiced affirmations to help rebuild my self-confidence. On the drive to work I'd call out things for which I was grateful. I even stated being grateful for having had this experience. I eliminated negativity. I refused to watch the national news stations, and I limited social media contact. I chose opportunities for laughter by going to Laughter Yoga

Clubs and watching comedies. But the most significant healing came when I reconnected with art. I sought opportunities to use visual art for self-expression. Painting was therapeutic because what I couldn't express in speech, I expressed through art. I started the journey of painting faces. I set up a makeshift art studio in my home office. I was eager to begin. Although I had tons of acrylic paint in the garage, I bypassed those dusty crates and made a mad dash to the local Walmart for some fresh new colors. I had a date with the arts and crafts section almost every other day.

In my office, there was paint everywhere! I was having the time of my life. I was having so much fun that I challenged myself to paint 100 faces. Finding Alignment and Co-creating for the Existence of that which you truly desire (FACE) simply means, connecting with God or your higher self and giving attention to what you want rather than what you don't want, to bring about the joys in life. This was the basis to my "100 FACES Project." To get started, I'd diffuse peppermint essential oil and put on some instrumental jazz music. I'd set an intention to trust that whatever image surfaced to the paper would have its own unique meaning. Each painting was created in three layers. The first layer allowed me to acknowledge the negative emotions that I was experiencing, and it provided a space for them to be released through written words. The second layer depicted painted symbols that covered those negative emotions. These symbols represented the emotions that were of service to me, unlike those in layer one, that evoked negative emotions. The face emerged with the third layer. Throughout this layering process, layer three revealed the total evolution of FACE. When the face was completed, I'd assign it an adjective and reflect on what it meant for me. The first image that surfaced was given the name *Humble*. It was healing to reflect on feeling humble for the opportunity for growth from this experience. Every face, from Number 1 to 20, had one thing in common, their eyes were closed. But there was something magical that happened with face Number 21. Unplanned, she appeared with her eyes open. She was given the name *Releasing*. *Releasing* gave me the power to let go of anything that no longer served me. This project is still in progress. To date, the last face completed is Number 43, which was given the name *Unlimited*. *Unlimited* reminds me that I get to choose how to experience opportunities. Painting has been the catalyst for my healing.

Whether you've experienced a personal or professional attack, your story is connected to your healing. Never think that your hardship is insignificant. By you standing in your truth, inadvertently others are permitted to do the same. The state of being occurs in every aspect of every day. When happiness become a choice, attacks are no longer welcome to disrupt our being. Powerful healing occurs when negative perspectives turn into a ***reason to be***. Remember happiness is always a choice.

Author Jo Ellen Reams

Jo Ellen Reams

Jo Ellen Reams is a native of Nash County, NC. She has been married to her soul mate, Joe Reams for 24 years. She has been blessed with a beautiful family, which includes her son, Justin and his wife Brandi (her daughter-in-love), and granddaughter, Bralee ("Miss B"), her daughter, Jessica Ellen and a chosen daughter, Alexia Hines. Her blessed family also includes her mother, father, brother, grandparents, aunts, uncles, niece, nephews and cousins. Jo Ellen worked as a Registered Nurse and specialized in diabetes. She obtained her Broker License in 2013 and became a REALTOR®.

Jo Ellen opened Keffer Reams Team Realty a real estate firm in 2017. She is a volunteer for Meal on Wheels and continues to serve her community in many capacities. She is a member of Fishing Creek Baptist Church, and also attends Christian Fellowship Church. Jo Ellen is a member of the Nash Rocky Mount Rotary, The Women's Professional Business Group, and Rocky Mount Small Business Group. She serves as a board member for Nash Community College Alumni Board. She is beginning a devotion and prayer online group called SHIFT (Sister's Healing in Faith Together) with her sister in Christ, Tasha Jones. She loves to garden, read, and spend time with her loved ones.

joellenreams@gmail.com
KefferReamsTeam.com
Facebook:
KefferReamsTeam /Realty@KefferReamsTeam or Jo Ellen Reams
Instagram: Jo Ellen Reams

Rise Above It, No Matter What

"**R**ise above it," I would always hear these three powerful words from my Meme. She would listen to everything I would tell her and then those three words would come. It didn't matter what the situation or whether I was right or wrong in the story. It was always the same, "**Rise above it**" with her finger pointed in the air. There were times I would say, "I'm tired of **Rising above it**" and she would smile and remind me of all the times we have failed our God. She would say, "We are to forgive just like Christ forgave us and then quote John 3:16- 17. *For God so loved the world that he gave his only begotten son that whosoever believeth in Him should not perish but have everlasting life. For God sent not his son into the world to condemn the world; but that the world through him might be saved.* She taught me that, **No Matter What,** you can always be kind. She taught me His word and lived a life of example. She was not without trials, tribulations, or trouble and neither shall we be. Christ says we will have all of that if we are called his children. I watched her faith soar in some heartbreaking times and I heard her prayers for all her loved ones. I watched her do her work and chores with a merry heart and tackle different seasons in life with so much grace. What a legacy she leaves for me and so many others. So much wisdom and so much pouring into my life, the life of my daughter, and many others. Where does that take us, you may ask?

Have you ever pondered why am I here? What am I supposed to do? Am I doing enough? Did I hear you correctly Lord? Is it supposed to be this way? Is it supposed to feel like this? What is my reason to be? I'm tired, I'm weary, and I'm worn. Why did you even create me? I want to quit. Why is it so hard? I can't do it anymore? Do any of these statements sound familiar? If you have ever said any of these statements or asked any of these questions, then we have some things in common because I have said them at times myself. I have a heart for those struggling with identity and the weight of feeling invisible, not good enough, not pretty enough, not the right size, not smart enough, not talented enough, and not fitting in. All the lies the enemy whispers to God's beautiful children that He created. I know the lies and listened to them far longer than I should. They are meant to kill your faith, steal your joy, and destroy what God has purposed you for. How do I know they are lies? The bible in John 8:44 tells us the enemy is a liar and the father of lies. He can't tell the truth. It also says **You Are Fearfully and Wonderfully Made-** Psalms 139:14. God's word is true and powerful and sharper than any two edged sword. God can't lie. We belong to the King of Kings and Lord of Lords and have royalty running through our veins. This should give us a call to **Rise No Matter What!** We are called to be his servants –serve others for his namesake. It's not about the status quo, finances, prestigious awards, titles, likes on Facebook, and all the other accolades we can earn. They are nice and well deserving and he blesses his children in many ways, but when the rubber meets the road and you are called to **Rise Above It,** what does that look like for you? When life takes your breath away and nothing feels like it will ever be okay again. When circumstances have occurred that weren't your fault. When that *terrible awful* happens. What then? What do we do? How do we respond; fear or faith? Do you believe God and trust His word? **Do you REALLY believe it?**

Do you trust when it doesn't feel good, when it feels like you can't breathe, when the wee hours of the night find you crying and full of anxiety, doubt, and guilt? Do you trust when you are confronted by All the things that are **NOT** from God? You see, I am writing this to share with you that heartache is heartache and pain is pain. It comes packaged differently for everyone, but the emotions we carry are the same. The enemy knows how to attack and what to use to try and stop us. The bible says he schemes to destroy us. He is our adversary not God's. My desire is for you to leave from reading this and know how to recognize the *Spirit* that is operating, so that you can use the tools God has given you. There is Power in our Praise. Do you lift a Hallelujah like the song and psalmist say? Do you praise God...**No Matter What**?

What if your **reason to be** is to raise a child to know and love the Lord? What if it's to pray and be a helpmate to a spouse that struggles with depression, rejection, or health issues? What if your reason to be is to be a chosen mother or father to a child that lost his parents? What if you are to encourage and care for the homeless? What if what you've been through is to help another struggling in the same circumstance? What if it's to care for aging parents? What if you were only born to be the person God chose to help lead just "one soul to Christ? What if it's to let God's love light shine through you to a lost hurt, dark world? God is asking us to trust him, believe him and look to him for everything **No Matter What!** No matter what life looks like or feels like, we are called to **Rise**! We are called and created for fellowship and relationship with our creator God and others. My calling is to be an encourager with a gift of compassion. To be a light and share Christ love. To pray that God will expose the enemy and teach others how to have true freedom in Christ. To be an example "**No Matter What"** life throws at us. We are all a work in progress. We will not be perfected until we receive our heavenly bodies. Faith moves God, Faith pleases God, and Faith is a gift from God. I heard a sermon not long ago and a profound statement was made – "We can't trust and control". How true!

No Matter What – whether you have finances or not, good health or not, relationship with your family or not, children rebelling, spouses leaving, loved ones with mental issues or addictions, friends that fall away or betray- Trust God and seek Him Put him above everything else and know that He is God. Praise Him through the storm **No Matter What**. Fight your battles on your knees, on your face. Give it to the only one that can save you from your troubles, from yourself –Jesus. Be a light; let others see who your God is so they will choose to ask him to be their Lord, too. Focus on heavenly language – Peace, Love, Kindness, Gentleness, Perseverance, Joy, Faith, and Patience. Focus on these things. Philippians 4:8 -*Whatever is true, whatever is noble, whatever is right, whatever is pure, whatever is lovely, whatever is admirable, if anything is excellent or praiseworthy think about such things*. Be quick to forgive - **No Matter What** we can always be kind. We are set apart. We are chosen. We are so loved.

I have learned: God is in the details. His word is alive and breathing and sharper than any two-edged sword.

I have learned: My weapons are Praise and Prayer.

I have learned: He puts the broken pieces back together.

I have learned: He makes a masterpiece out of our messes.

I have learned: Even when we feel alone - He is always with us – He promises to never leave us nor forsake us – we are not in control – God is.

I have learned: As long as there is breath there is hope.

Trials, tribulations, and sufferings will come, but God works it all out for our good.- Romans 8:28

He controls my destiny and no devil can take my last breath. God gave us our breath and God determines when our work is done.

Joy comes from the Lord; the maker of heaven and earth. Not our circumstances.

I have learned: His mercies are new every morning. We are not perfect and He is willing to forgive us. I often "get in my feelings" and often have to ask for forgiveness.

I have learned: To recognize the voice that is speaking and the spirit that is operating. To put on the Gospel Amour and never take it off.

I have learned: To praise Him no matter what!

I have learned: He fights our battles.

I have learned: To speak Life over your situations, loved ones and yourself. Power is in the words you use.

I have seen miracles from God with my own eyes. Do we love Him for what he can do for us *OR* because of who *He* is?

When we are tired, weary or worn and our hearts are broken – **Rest** in God and stand on His word – He **WILL** give you **Rest. Then Rise** to your calling – walk worthy of it. He will lift you and equip you with everything you need – Trust and obey for His promises are true. What does God say about you and who you are? Whose report are you going to believe – God's or man's? I choose to cling to a scripture he gave me recently during an extremely difficult and heartbreaking time. *God is within her and she will NOT fall. God will help her at the break of day.-* (Psalm 46:5) *For I, says the Lord, will be a wall of fire all around her, and I will be the Glory in her midst.-* (Zechariah 2:1-5.) Those verses right there should put a pep in your step. They sure did for me. I choose to continue to stand on God's promises and to claim them He will give you exactly what you need when you need it, to face any obstacle. He has promised that He is with you always and He orders our steps. He never sleeps and it never takes him by surprise. His promises are true. **His promises will be the Rest in the Rise.** Rest in His word. Rest in His presence. Rest your mind. Just Rest. Be still and know.... Rest under the shelter of His Almighty wings. So I say again, I will praise Him all the days of my life and when I no longer have breath I will praise Him forevermore. I long to hear "Enter, well done thy good and faithful servant."

Please understand I get that we will all have tears and moments that take our breath away. We will feel drained, and at times it can be difficult to even pray or ask God for anything. It will be a process. God is right there in the trenches with you. He is going to take you from the *Pit to the Palace.* There is a purpose for your pain and he collects every tear. Our names are written on the palms of His hands. Fight the good fight of faith and run the race set before you. To God be all the Glory.

My Meme transitioned to be with the Lord on January 19, 2017 and my heart is still missing her. She had spoken of that day many times and I would always stop her. I just couldn't bear the thought of it. Life is different now and it has taken me awhile to breathe again. I never could have truly been prepared for the hole in my heart and the world that her transitioning created. God sent me a dear Sister-in-Christ to give me some words of wisdom. She said, "You don't have a hole. You have a well. A well that is filled and will never run dry and when you need to know she is there you just pull from that well that runs so deep. She has passed the mantle to you. Her work is done and now it is time for yours to continue." So as I conclude, I pray I can be as wise and faithful as I watched her be. I pray I age gracefully and always praise my God. I pray I seek forgiveness when I have sinned. I pray this touches something inside of you and helps you during difficult seasons in your life and that you too will have a song of praise on your lips. I pray if you haven't asked him to be your Saviour that you won't wait and that you will repent of your sins, believe He sent Jesus to die for your sins and that he rose from the grave, and confess that He is Lord and ask Him to be Lord of your life. The King is coming and time is drawing near. Please give your life to Him so that you may inherit eternal salvation. To God be All the Glory, Power, Dominion, Forever and Ever. Amen and Amen.

In love and Honor of my heartbeat, "My Meme" (grandmother) Conway "Lois" Murray. December 19, 1919 to January 19, 2017.

A REASON TO BE

He who has a why to live for can bear almost any how.

~ Friedrich Nietzsche

A REASON TO BE VOLUME 3

Author Dr. Marvin Smith

Dr. Marvin Smith

Dr. Marvin E. Smith, better known as Bishop or Apostle, is truly a man after God's own heart. A native of Pinetops, North Carolina, Bishop Smith is a veteran of the US Army.

Bishop Smith began his voyage of ministry as a young man. He later became a Bishop to churches across the nation. His words of wisdom, gift of knowledge, and the spirit of understanding have inspired many.

A Reason To Be: Creativity & Innovation

God is the one who gives gifts to men and women such as creativity. Faith in GOD - Empowered by His WORD and belief in yourself through Christ and your business vision or ministry vision are essential to long term success. (Everything is spiritual) -Creativity burst from within; from spirit to stir our hearts and minds with newness and possibilities of Expanding our Vision and purpose. Creativity is mastery of giving physical manifestation to dreams not yet realized. Creativity is the breath that empowers and gives life to our everyday moments and gives glory to our Creator, God. You must fan the flames and keep the fire burning. Whatever it takes, pray God's Word, praise, and worship; connecting with other like- minded people. Keep the flame of creativity burning and rekindled. We have to be intentional in reviving the gifts in our lives, and use them constantly, so they can explode like a volcano and erupt and change the landscape. The Word of God says, "Stir up the Gift". The Milne Greek Word in reference to 'stir up the gift of God, 'is anazo'pureo', which means, to kindle anew, rekindle or resuscitate, in context of a fire."

"Therefore I remind you stir, (fan into flames) the gift of God, which is in you by laying on of my hands. For God has not given us the spirit of fear, but power, and love and self-control."(II Tim 1:6-7)

"Stir up (rekindle the embers of, fan the flame of, and keep burning the (gracious) gift of God (the inner fire) that is in you....." Amplified Bible. The gift in this verse refers to a spiritual gift that edifies, builds up and encourages the church by empowering the individuals to share God's work with others, both believers and unbelievers. Timothy's spiritual gift was already within him and part of his faith as were the spiritual gifts of his mother and grandmothers.

Starting a business or ministry is a spiritual journey.

So you need the breath of God's WORD for good and tough times. Solomon didn't ask for wealth but for a wise and understanding heart, God granted that and more to him. God has given each one of us certain gifts of creativity. It is up to us to discover them and then put them to use for His glory. God never asks us to do something that He doesn't give us the ability to do. So each of us have been equipped by our Creator to have gifting in specific areas, even as He has given each member of the Body of Christ gifts of the Spirit. My desire is to stir up the gift in and be set on fire with and fan the flames in others so they may burn with fervent passion in their purpose; being creative with new ideas to empower others to the glory of God! God wants us to prosper. *"But remember the LORD your GOD, for it is He who gives you the ability to produce wealth, and so confirms His covenant, which He swore to your ancestors, as it is today." Deuteronomy 8:18 (NIV).* All of our skills and talents that we use belong to God. He gives us the ability to make money and negotiate deals.

Creativity and Innovation is a mindset

"Do not conform to the pattern of this world, but be transformed by the renewing of your mind." Romans 12:2. Then you will be able to test and approve what God's will is; His Will is good, pleasing and perfect. We must be learners for a lifetime; reading constantly, partnering with the right people, embracing mentors and understanding the demand for better products- cars didn't end with the invention of the Model T Ford. So we should never rest on our success; we should seek to innovate and improve. The Bible commands us to be Creative and Innovative in our businesses. Be yourself an original and not a copy.

Creativity is Related to Imagination; But Innovation is Related to Implementation

The primary difference between creativity and innovation is that creativity refers to conception of a fresh idea or plan, whereas innovation implies initiating something new to the market, which has not been introduced previously. We can learn to operate on the cutting edge! Having an edge gives you an upper hand!!

Consider these definitions:

Creativity (UNMEASURABLE IMAGINATIVE PROCESS) - generate new ideas, alternatives, solutions, and possibilities in a unique and different way. The ability to conceive something unpredictable, original and unique. It must be expressive, exciting and imaginative. Creativity is a brainstorming and mind-blogging activity in which a person has to think beyond his imagination for something worthwhile and better for the market. It is an activity of unveiling, or putting in reality, something which was previously hidden. Creativity does not require money and has no risks factors, so DREAM BIG!

Innovation (PRODUCTIVE PROCESS)- introducing something better into the market. The act of the application of *new ideas* which creates some value for a business, organization, government, and society as well. A better and smarter way of doing something is innovation.

Innovation married to Creativity - putting creative ideas into measurable action. The outcome should be positive; bearing fruit and fruit remaining! It is the process of doing something better for the first time, which was not done by anyone else. A change bringing a new edge to the performance and productivity of the business, organization, government or ministry. Innovation requires money and a risk factor. THERE IS A PRICE FOR SUCCESS!

"See, the Lord has called by name Bezalel the son of Uri, son of Hur, of the tribe of Judah; and he has filled him with the Spirit of God, with skill, with intelligence, with knowledge, and with all-craftsmanship, to devise artistic designs, to work in gold and silver and bronze, in cutting stones for setting, and in carving wood, for work in every skilled craft." (Exodus 35:30-33)

Bezalel was given gifts and talents to work in a creative manner on the building of the tabernacle of God. These creative abilities included understanding, knowledge, and skill in his craft. God expected Bezalel to pass along these abilities and so He *"inspired him to teach, both him and Oholiab the son of Ahisamach of the tribe of Dan. He has filled them with skills to do every sort of work done by an engraver or by a designer or by an embroiderer in blue and purple and scarlet yarn and fine twined linen, or by a weaver—by any sort of workman or skilled designer" (Exodus 35:34-35)*. It was the Lord that gave Bezalel these creative gifts and God expected him to teach these skills to others.

"For by grace you have been saved through faith; and not of yourself, it is the gift of God; not as a result of works, that no one should boast. For we are his workmanship, created in Christ Jesus for good works, which God prepared beforehand that we should walk in them." (Ephesians 2:8-10) Paul declares the creativity of God here in both creation and redemption. We are God's workmanship, literally 'a work of art" (Greek- *poiema* from which we get the word poem). We are then called to continue on God's creative works for the benefit of others.

The Spirit of God empowers us to be creative and innovative. We are imitators of God. We are created in His likeness. (Genesis 1:2) We are to be like Him. This means we are designed to be creative, too. You have a unique contribution to make in this life. When we look at who God is and what He has done, we have a **Reason To Be** creative - through entrepreneurship, the arts, inventions, or solutions to everyday problems. It gives glory back to God, who created us in his image!

It is high time to unleash our creative potential and use it to communicate and display the God-given purpose in our life, Creativity is not an option; it is a biblical mandate that flows from the will of God. We must not only create but innovate... not just manage the existing but innovate the new and the different. As leaders, we must work on tomorrow, not just keep up with today. That is what innovation is all about.

Creative thinking is not a talent; it is a skill that can be learned. It empowers people by adding strength to natural abilities which improves teamwork, productivity and delivers appropriate profits.

Creativity is one of the most important resources. We serve a creative God who, though He never changes in His character, has designed a world full of variety and freshness.

We must think outside the box. Creating an atmosphere among family and teams that says, "Let's find a better way." Always look for a new idea that will improve or expand your business or ministry. Note the creativity in this scripture:

"A few days later, when Jesus again entered Capernaum, the people heard that he had come home. They gathered in such large numbers that there was no room left, not even outside the door, and he preached the word to them. Some men came, bringing to him a paralyzed man, carried by four of them. Since they could not get him to Jesus because of the crowd, they made an opening in the roof above Jesus by digging through it and then lowered the mat the man was lying on. When Jesus saw their faith (creativity and innovation) he said to the paralyzed man, "Son, your sins are forgiven." (Mark 2:1-5)

Even frustration is a catalyst to innovation. The crowd forced the men to innovate and think outside the box to get the paralyzed man to Jesus. Being willing to take the risk of failure is twin to realize success. "Success is on the far side of failure."

Just as with Bezalel, we are God's workmanship and we were created for the purpose of glorifying God in good works. These works were "prepared beforehand" for us, so "that we should walk in them" or so that we should do good things for Christ. The church is called the Body of Christ. We are to be His hands, feet, voice, eyes, and to be a body doing as Christ would be doing if He was here in His physical presence on earth. He is the Head and we are to be His Body and as His body, we are to be doing what He has sovereignly appointed us to do, our **Reason To Be.** We were created as His workmanship to be working in the lives of others.

"Behold, I give you a wise and discerning mind, so that none like you has been before you and none like you shall arise after you." (I King 3:12) Solomon could have asked for wealth, he could have asked for power, but Solomon asked for wisdom and a discerning mind and God honored that request, saying that there would be "none like you" who has been so wise as him, either before or after him "so that no other king shall compare with you, all your days" (I Kings 3:13b). Since Solomon asked for something more valuable than riches, God promised to give him a long life. (I King*s 3:14) and "both riches and honor" II Kings 3:13a).*

"Do you see a man skillful in his work? He will stand before kings; he will not stand before obscure men." (Proverbs 22:29) A man or woman who is skillful in his or her work will not go unnoticed by the Lord. Just to have a skill is one thing, but to use it in their work is altogether different and those who have such creative skills will be noticed by God and "will not stand before obscure men" meaning that they'll be noticed by those in the world as well. A talent that is buried is useless but a skill that is utilized displays the glory of God who gives to all, uncommon abilities, talents, and creative skills.

"Do not neglect the gift you have, which was given you by prophecy when the council of elders laid their hands on you. Practice these things, immerse yourself in them, so that all may see your progress. (I Timothy 4:14-15) This scripture speaks concerning gifting for God and importation for man by God's Spirit. Paul tells Timothy and us, that a gift can be neglected if it's not utilized. We must share our gift of creativity. The idea in these verses is that this gift must be

utilized and the person must submerge themselves in their use of them. When they do, "all may see [our] outcome" and can be helped and may glorify God Who is the giver of all good gifts of creativity. Corinthians 9:24. Do you not know that in a race all runners run, but only one gets the prize? Run in such a way as to get the prize. Running a business is tough. It's a marathon not a sprint. You stumble and make mistakes along the way. But when you fall, it is said and I quote "winners get up faster than anyone else. You do what you need to do to win." Maybe you need to catch a second wind!

Jesus said to them, *"Don't be afraid; just believe." (Mark 5:36)* There are times when you are the only person who believes in your business dream. Take courage like Joshua and be very strong and believe in God and yourself and in your business idea or ministry vision.

"Whatever you do, work heartily, as for the Lord and not for men, knowing that from the Lord you will receive the inheritance as your reward. You are serving the Lord Christ." (Colossians 3:23-24)

Author Sheila Patrice Spencer

Author Sheila Patrice Spencer

With a passion for writing, storytelling, ministry, and spoken word, Rev. Sheila P. Spencer is committed to educating, encouraging and empowering people. Delivering a global perspective, she is an esteemed Director of Education, published author, and contributing columnist to the Spiritual Outlook section of the *Indianapolis Recorder*. Sheila's published works include *Unto Whom Much is Given* and *From the Jewelry Box: Custom Made Inspiration*. Sheila's work is also featured in the *Chicken Soup for the African American Woman's Soul* anthology. In addition, she has recorded a Spoken Word CD and an audio version of her books. Rev Sheila Spencer is a Southern California transplant.

You can learn more about her at www.sheilapspencer.com.

Take The Leap and Let Go

I was about to do something on my bucket list. When I was done, I would be able to put a check next to ... skydiving. I purposely did not tell some of my friends because it was not what they expected; I knew they would think I was crazy and try to talk me out of it. It was the day of the skydive and we had just completed our required orientation. During the session, we learned that most of the staff had skydived. As we prepared, I asked one of the staff members, "What's the scariest part about jumping out of the plane?" My friend responded before the staff person could speak, "Okay, Sheila - You know that your question just answered your question?! What is the scariest thing about jumping out of a plane? Jumping out of a plane!" Meanwhile, the staff person thought for a moment and said, "Well, I wouldn't necessarily describe it as scary ... but pay attention to what happens to you the moment before you leap and let go."

The moment before you let go ....

Her words remained with me as we boarded the tiny airplane. We ascended 5,000, 10,000, 15,000 feet in the air and beyond. My instructor was reviewing the directions with me as we were preparing for the leap. It was the moment before I was going to leap and let go. My instructor said, "Sheila, before we leap, you have to be still for a few seconds. Now, I want you to create a visual image for yourself."

It is the moment right before the leap. Even though I am still seated in the plane, my feet are literally hanging out in the air. Half of me is on the plane and the other half is off. I know it was a few seconds, but it felt like forever. My body was in this unnatural holding pattern. I was frozen between the comfort of the known confines of the small plane and the other half was in the unknown and limitless sky. It was as if my body was screaming "Sheila- Patrice-Spencer, I was NOT created to be suspended between this known and unknown! Either get back on the plane or leap forward and let go – but either way you have to make a decision!"

It was at that moment my instructor said, "Sheila, are you ready?" In that moment, I wasn't ready. I was completely terrified, yet my response was "Let's do this!"

And I leaped.

Initially, I was holding on to the parachute straps so tightly, I could *feel* my instructor telling me, "Sheila, let go and open up your arms. You need to completely surrender in order to enjoy the whole experience."

I let go and surrendered and it was AMAZING.

As I soared through the limitless sky, I realized that I would have missed all of this beauty and wonder if I did not take the leap. I was able to view the world through a different perspective and point of view. All of this was waiting for me on the other side of my leap. It was amazing. When I landed on the ground, I realized I could have stayed on the plane and arrived at the same place. However, I would have missed the joy of the *journey* of the leap.

As we drove back, I reflected. How often are we walking around in this frozen, suspended state between the known comfort of holding on and the unknown discomfort of letting go? Half of us connected to the comfort and the other half in the midst of a limitless unknown. How often have I lived for years paralyzed in comfort; while my spirit screamed out for me to let go?

Here are three lessons that skydiving taught me about letting go:

1. **Letting go takes courage, yet that does not mean you don't do it afraid.** It takes courage to let go and surrender. Whether it is a new assignment, relationship or opportunity, it is normal to be scared. Courage does not mean having no fear; courage calls us to do it in spite of fear. A friend shared that if your dream doesn't scare you a little bit, maybe it is not big enough. Remember, it takes courage to let go of the familiar and embrace the new.

2. **Letting go releases you from expectations**. I tend to be a planner. We plan our lives and schedule when we plan to reach certain milestones. There are our pre-set expected dates when we will graduate, start our careers, begin our families, purchase our cars, buy our homes and retire. But what happens when you do not accomplish the milestone by your expected date? We are imprisoned by our own expectations; remaining paralyzed because it did not go as we expected. Letting go means surrendering. It reminds us that the life we scheduled is not always the life that God has planned for us. We must be willing to let go of the life we planned to have the life that is waiting for us. Letting go frees you from being stuck when life doesn't go as expected.

Letting go liberates us from the expectations of others and our own expectations of ourselves.

3. **Letting go opens up new possibilities** – When I leaped, I opened myself up to a breathtaking experience that was waiting for me. Letting go opens you up to new perspectives and expands your life. Several years ago, I had a comfortable life in California. I was writing, teaching and surrounded by the familiar life of family and friends. Suddenly, a job opportunity came that would allow me to write, travel, teach, and interact with people all over the world. However, the position would require me to move to Indianapolis, Indiana. There is a season between fall and spring called winter. It is cold in the winter. There is snow during this season. Sheila does not do cold.

I purposely did not tell some of my friends because it was not what they expected; they would think I was crazy and they would try to talk me out of it. When God gives you a vision, it is not always meant for you to share it with everyone.

However, in the midst of this transition, my friend sent me a card with a beautiful quote from Anais Nin - "The day came when the risk to remain tight in the bud was more painful than the risk it took to blossom."

After prayer, I called my colleague with my decision. This literally was my response, "I am completely terrified, don't know what to expect and have no idea how things are going to work out. But I am letting go of all that to take this leap and accept the job." I accepted the position because the risk of remaining comfortable was more painful than the risk of letting go. However, there was a reward on the other side of the leap. If I did not leap, I never would have met my sister, Amanda from Colombia or connected with my sister, Rosette from the

Democratic Republic of the Congo. My life would not have been impacted by the countless lives who have blessed me through travel.

    Letting go removed me from my comfort zone and allowed me to experience God in a new way and deepen my relationship. There were lifelong friendships that were waiting for me on the other side of the leap. Joy, tears, heartache and love were waiting on the other side of the leap. Authoring a book and music were waiting on the other side of the leap. This preacher's daughter left California and was able to completely acknowledge the ministry call on my own life. I graduated from seminary and was ordained in Indiana. This ministry will reflect the authenticity of who I am and is letting go of the expectations that it will look like my father's ministry. Writing this chapter was waiting for me on the other side of the leap.

Letting go takes courage, but it does not mean you do not do it afraid.
Take the leap and let go.
Letting go releases you from expectations.
Take the leap and let go.
Letting go opens up new possibilities.
Take the leap and let go.

    There is another lesson from my leap. Before I took the leap, my instructor told me, "Sheila, remember I am attached to you. When you jump out of the plane, I am with you because we are connected. Even if you don't hear me, remember that I am with you throughout the whole experience." When we let go and surrender, God is with us.

"Haven't I commanded you? Strength! Courage! Don't be timid; don't get discouraged. God, your God, is with you every step you take." (Joshua 1:9) There are treasures, books, projects, businesses, visions, ministries and relationships that are waiting for you on the other side of your leap. There are people who are waiting to be blessed by your gifts and presence on the other side of your surrender. There are limitless possibilities waiting for you outside of your comfort zone. It is worth the leap and a reason to be willing to let go.

It's time for another transition in my life and I feel as if I am in the small airplane as it ascends into the air. I am sitting on the edge of the plane and I know it's time to leap and I am nervous. But when I think about the possibilities that are on the other side of my surrender ... I take the leap and let go.

It is amazing. Take the Leap!

Rev. Sheila P. Spencer

Author Jacqueline Thompson

Jacqueline Thompson

Jacqueline Thompson is a passionate servant leader with a BOSS Status Approach (Being One Smart Sister – Totally Equipped). The Author of *Broken and Embracing the Journey.* Co-Author of the *Diary of a People Pleaser,* compiled by Cheryl Peavy and Co-Author of, *The Great Bounce Back,* compiled by Rebecca Huggins. Jacqueline has a passion, drive and purpose to write! In addition to her love for writing, Jacqueline also enjoys serving others as a Writing Coach, Life Focus Coach, Mentor, Editor, Ghost Writer, and Graphics Designer. By day, she is a full-time Technical Expert, leading the way in technology. She recently founded *Penned Just Write, LLC* which specializes in helping others share their voice and designs; boldly, courageously, and with confidence in their unique way. Jacqueline has spoken on several social media platforms. She has also served as a panelist at women's conferences and as a guest on radio shows to share her experiences; presenting titled sessions such as- *People Pleaser, Embracing the Beauty in Brokenness,* and *Failing Forward.* Jacqueline is passionate about helping others express their truth, see brokenness as a God-experience and live the best version of their lives. What are her next goals? Completing a 365-Day Focus Journal, finalizing an e-Book on *BOSS Status: Being One Smart Sister – Totally Equipped* and developing a Virtual Writing Workshop.

Jacqueline is a devoted wife and mother, and *Mimi* to four amazing grandchildren. She is a native of Chicago, Illinois. and currently resides in Charlotte, North Carolina. You can connect with her on all social media platforms under Jacqueline Thompson, Penned Just Write, or by visiting her website at: www.pennedjustwrite.com.

A Perfect Ending

I am wonderfully and masterfully created by God. Accepting this was an *ah ha* moment during my season of discovering self-love and discovering that a relationship with God was what was missing in my life. I was almost fifty years old before I understood that God does not make mistakes. Finally, I took those words to heart. Becoming a woman of God didn't come easy for me because I couldn't fathom exposing my true identity. People-pleasing was my way of life, and it took a long while for me to get to a place of accepting myself as I was. From childhood to adulthood, I lived a life of deception. Early in my life, no one had taught me that truth was more accepted than deception. More than anything, I wanted to be loved and accepted. No one told me that I didn't have to become someone else; hiding behind a mask and using deception to get that love and acceptance. I would tell people anything to get them to like me, love me and accept me. When I started to make my own money, I would even give them material possessions, trying to win their friendship or love. Finally, truth won out. My *reason to be* came from embracing my season of brokenness. In my new season, I love telling others how my brokenness turned out to be a beautiful gift that God wanted me to experience. Had it not been for my brokenness, how else would God be able to use me as a vessel to reveal my life to others? Take this journey with me as I share with you what it was like to frivolously live life on my own and much later discover that without God, I'm nothing. But, oh how God expresses His love, turning our *ashes into beauty!*

Our Plan Sucks!

Life was okay for me; or so I thought. I packed up my things and was the first out of eleven siblings to venture out to discover a new life away from Chicago. Moving to Atlanta to find a better life for my two small children was adventurous, courageous and a journey I traveled alone. I thought I had it all planned out because I wanted to get out of Chicago and leave the hurt of failures, disappointments and a lack of integrity behind me. I wanted to start over and prove to myself that I could regain success, happiness and honesty in my life. I felt that moving to a new city where no one knew me was that perfect opportunity to get it right without judgement. I wanted to believe that *this was my second chance.*

I had dropped out of high school and married as a virgin at eighteen years old. I married my husband to get out of my parents' home, but never once thought about the commitment that comes with marriage. My husband and I were separated more than we were married, and I regretted getting married so early in my adult life. I felt like I was missing so much and became very deceitful in where I was going, who I was with and how my money was being spent. I finally became pregnant after seven years of being in and out of this marriage and within a year of our daughter being born, I was ready to leave! However, my husband and I, somehow managed to remain together because of our daughter and my son, who was conceived through a one-night stand with another man. Although I believed my husband genuinely loved my son, I felt the resentment he had towards me and this was my clue that it was time to put my plan into action. We legally separated and I moved back home with my parents while I saved up enough money to make that move to Atlanta. Life was becoming too much for me to handle and I needed a change of scenery.

Before I left Chicago and headed to Atlanta, I had lost many friendships due to betrayal. My daughter was two years old and my son was six months old at the time, and my plan was to secure a better life for them. However, because of my uncertainty, I decided to leave my children with my parents until I settled in. I can remember how beautiful the new city was and how welcoming people made me feel. It was easy landing a great job and I looked forward to what this new life would bring for me and my family. My daughter soon joined me, but my son stayed with my parents. I can't tell you why I made that decision, but I know that it was one of many poor decisions I made on this journey. My plan was interrupted when I met another young man. He was tall, handsome and had the most beautiful eyes. We immediately hit it off and became a couple in less than a week. I can't explain the attraction that kept me in this relationship, but I knew it was time to finalize my divorce from my first husband so that I could marry this new man in my life. Although our relationship was dysfunctional and disrespectful, I married him before giving birth to our second son. Our life was fast, competitive and filled with sinful behaviors, but we kept trying to make it work

I had several decent and high paying jobs. I'm talking about jobs that one would normally only get after successfully graduating from college. Unfortunately, due to my lack of integrity, I could not hold on to any of these jobs. We moved from place to place because we couldn't pay our rent on time, was lousy in managing our money, and reckless in our spending habits. Life was about driving fancy cars, buying expensive, name brand everything, discovering the best wines, socializing with my friends, attending happy-hour events and splurging on others. After eleven years of domestic abuse, initiated by both of us, our marriage ended on a very bitter note. I lost custody of our sons; my children were all separated and my initial plans of making a better life for me and my children was another failed part of my journey.

Edging God Out

So, you think you know everything, huh? You think you know how to solve your own problems, be successful on your own, deal with your marital issues on your own, raise your kids on your own, have successful relationships on your own, manage your money on your own and live life on your own. Yes! I thought I knew it all. This was the mindset I had most of my life. Yes, I knew of God and I knew about His Son, Jesus that was sent to save our sinful ways and that Jesus fulfilled his purpose to leave us a helper to guide us through life. What I didn't have was *a solid relationship* with God, Jesus and the Holy Spirit. I lacked that relationship with the Holy Spirit that could teach me the significance of why having that relationship with Him would give Him total control over my life. I was rebellious and never worked on having a relationship with Him because I didn't think I needed Him. I only thought that knowing Him was enough. I never got to a point of reverencing Him as my source or His Word as my blueprint for life. I was comfortable figuring it out all on my own, yet very confused as to why I would end up in an all-to-familiar place, one too many times. Same type of men in and out of my life. Same financial blow-ups in my life. Same poor relationships with friends and family members. Same career mistakes every single time. Same losses of the same material possessions over and over and over again. Same people-pleasing mentality so that people would like, love and accept me as someone I was not. One would think that after being bailed out of these very uncomfortable situations more than twenty times (and I'm not exaggerating) that I would have by now, gotten my act together. Oh, but I got this, right? Wrong! I never had it and continued to think that by relying on myself, I would eventually get it right. One thing I know for sure is that when we *Edge God Out,* we are relying on our own *EGO* to get through this life and we're going about it the wrong way!

Broken has a Purpose

Everything I tried to do on my own had a *purpose!* I remember being in what would not be the last episode of a broken moment in my life. I was working for a major airline and was doing well in my career. I was single and very happy that I could afford to lease a beautiful two-story home right outside of Atlanta. Our sons were living with their dad and it made me proud to give them another home to come to whenever they wanted to. I had been promoted and was in the running for another promotion when that day happened. I was called into the office and questioned about the family members on my flight list. Shocked at the fact I was selectively chosen to question, I began to lie about it all, in an attempt to keep my job. I knew that one of the family members on my flight list was not my biological son but went through loops trying to prove that he was, to keep my job. The thoughts racing through my head were: *"I just got a new home and I'm up for a new promotion. There's no way I'm going to mess this up. I won't expose the fact that I allowed others to talk me into putting someone not related to me on my flight list of family members and that this cannot be happening to me again".* I should have learned my lesson a long time ago about the fallacy of pleasing others; but I hadn't and because I stuck to the deceit, instead of revealing the truth, I ended up losing my job. I remember going home that day and crying until I couldn't cry anymore. I yearned for God's love during that dark moment.

But it was Good for Me

My entire life up until I discovered my purpose, I was kept by God's mercy. He allowed me to go through life on my own and started breaking me early. I just didn't notice it. He tried time and time again to get my attention, but I wasn't listening. I didn't care about what He had to say and breaking me to my core was the only way He could get my attention the way that He needed to. After crying my heart out, I knew that I had to work on a survival plan because I wanted to keep my home. When I discovered that it was going to take longer than I expected, I knew that I had to find a plan B. I was unemployed and I had no way to pay my bills. My plan B was to sell everything in my home except a few things and head back to the one place I knew I would be welcomed! Momma's house!

It really hurt to tell my landlords that I was not going to be able to keep the home that they went out of their way to lease to me. This was their first rental property and it was less than two years old. They trusted the referral from a mutual friend and leased the home to me. They were one of the nicest couples I had ever known. Although they empathized with my situation, I could tell that they were not happy that I had been in the home for less than six months and was breaking the lease. This meant that they had to put the home back on the market again. I had less than two weeks to leave; yet my landlords promised to not put it on my record as breaking the lease. Those two weeks crept on me fast, and I didn't have enough time to sell my belongings, so I gave away everything to one of my friend's son who was just moving into his first apartment. I didn't care about the money or anything at this time. I just wanted to get to my Mom!

As I was packing the things that I was taking with me, I discovered a book by Charles Stanley, called -*God Is In Control* and I remember shedding tears that dampened the pages as I read the book, in my now, empty home. I didn't have any money and my friend brought me a bus ticket from Atlanta to Arkansas. I cried when I saw my mom and I thought she would be judgmental about my situation, but she was the total opposite. She embraced me in my sadness and told me that God would work it all out and I believed her.

I diligently looked for work and was becoming discouraged that no one was calling me after about a month of unemployment. I didn't give up hope and tried my best to remain positive. When the calls started coming in, I had three offers on the table but was only interested in one because it would put me back into the field of technology which I had now, been out of for some years. It would also bring me closer to my two sons who resided in Atlanta. I prayed about this job and when they flew me to Atlanta for the interview, I was confident that the interview was successful. Two weeks had passed by and still no word from this company. The other two were still offers on the table, but I wasn't feeling either of them the way I was feeling the technology position. So I prayed and asked God to show me which job He wanted me to have.

I remember the day so clearly. It was Good Friday when the call came in, and I could feel butterflies in my stomach as I answered the phone. It was the technology company offering me the job! I jumped for joy because it was the job I wanted. It was in my area of expertise, the pay was great and it was back in Atlanta. I worked hard to complete my training certification which was a requirement before I was working solo as a Technical Trainer. I was determined to succeed and was traveling all over the United States training clients on our pharmaceutical software. During one of our training sessions at the corporate office in Atlanta, I allowed a racial slur from a colleague to upset me and I said something to him about it that he didn't like. Little did I know that he was very close to my immediate supervisor. My final training session was in Albuquerque, New Mexico, and my supervisor gave me rave reviews about the client's comments about my training. We had dinner and my supervisor informed me that I had now passed the certification program. I went home and celebrated with my new husband and was looking forward to starting my first day as a solo Technical Trainer. I drove from Arkansas to Atlanta in my new car and was looking forward to telling my sons about the good news. When I arrived at work Monday morning, I thought I was being called into the Office of the Director to be congratulated on my success, but discovered that I was being *released* for several reasons; my reaction towards my colleague who made a racial slur towards me, leaving my laptop behind during one of our meetings in Detroit, and dropping and losing my American Express Card while boarding a plane. Her reasons were that she didn't feel like I was taking my job seriously. I stood there in shock from what I was hearing. Then I was required to turn in my laptop and badge and I was escorted out of the building.

    A growth moment: "Really God? What just happened and why?" I sat in my car for at least an hour and cried before calling my husband to give him the news. I didn't call my sons; I drove eight hours back to Arkansas! It was good for me! The drive gave me time to connect with God and losing my job was another broken moment where God needed my attention. He got it!

My Reason to Be!

My Reason to Be is a perfect ending to a journey of brokenness, people-pleasing, deception, and loss. I've bounced back from it all and can only thank my Heavenly Father for not giving up on me and enabling me to not give up on myself. Losing that last job was a defining moment. I could have reverted back to a life of *Edging God Out* or I could have said, "I don't know what just happened, but *God, You're in Control.* Give me strength to get through this and an understanding of what You want me to learn from this". I choose the latter approach and determined that I would not live without God another day in life! Am I where I want to be in life? Absolutely not; but I am where I need to be. I'm walking in my *purpose* and enjoying every moment of it. I'm not making the salary I once had; however, I have discovered my *passion* in life. When *passion* and *purpose* are in sync, you know that God's hand is all over you. I'm not perfect but my *purpose* is. *My Reason to Be* is a part of my journey that I'm joyful about. A part of my journey was the discovery that I love writing about my experiences. I strongly believe that sharing my story can make a difference in someone else's life. What's your reason to be? Is there a part of you that you can share with others to make a difference? None of us are perfect in life, but we do have a *perfect purpose*! Find yours and watch God use *you* as the vessel He created you to be!

A REASON TO BE

Meet The Visionary: Author Tilda Whitaker

Tilda Whitaker has mentored and coached thousands to assist and achieve their life purpose through her 501c3 nonprofit organization which has been recognized nationally and internationally and her company, P4 Coaching Institute. Tilda trains extensively to help leaders plan, process and produce with purpose to create legacies globally. Her message is set to compel the attention of those who seek to discover their purpose in life and launch their destiny. She is credential by the International Coach Federation (ICF) as a Professional Certified Coach (PCC); she is presently an ICF member, Pastor of Soul Winners International Ministries- "SWIM"

P4 Coaching Institute™

PLAN, PROCESS & PRODUCE WITH PURPOSE

WWW.P4CINSTITUTE.COM

"Equipping nonprofit & ministry leaders to plan, process & produce with purpose to create legacies globally"
P4 Coaching Institute offers certification for Certified Professional Life Coach and Certified Christian Mentor. The ICF accredited program is designed and delivered onsite or online.

ACSTH
Approved Coach Specific Training Hours
International Coach Federation

SHERO PUBLISHING

Empowering The World, One Book At A Time

Sheropublishing.com

Made in the USA
Columbia, SC
08 September 2019